ADVANCE REVIEWS

Navigating life's Journey is a beautifully written and impassioned plea to follow one's dreams using the roadmap that has been set forth by those who've gone before. This magnificent retrospective on how to utilize lessons already learned to blaze a trail to happiness and success is full of great examples of how to make the most of your journey – though it won't always be easy. A "must-read" for those trying to navigate their own "river" of life."

– Joe Coleman, former lead singer of The Platters and member of Voices of Classic Soul

Written In the midst of a global pandemic when the entire world is on edge, Richard Battle delivers unforgettable lessons that will prepare you for the inevitable twists and turns of life. Through the combination of powerful stories, inspirational quotes, and meaningful parables, Richard provides Americans with a blueprint for excellence in an hour when we need it most.

– Jonathan Jakubowski, Author of *Bellwether Blues, A Conservative Awakening of the Millennial Soul*

Has there ever been a timelier book than *'Navigating Life's Journey: Common Sense in Uncommon Times'* by Richard Battle than now in our nation's history? We've had the great fortune to assist with Richard's many appearances on television, radio, print, and online outlets. I believe there's a very good reason why Richard is in high demand-what he has to say makes sense, when little else seems to in today's world. When common sense is in short supply, Richard Battle is your guy.

- Burke Allen, Chief Media Strategist, Allen Media Strategies Washington, DC - www.allenmediastrategies.com.

Richard's latest book about navigating life's journey should be a valuable and profound contribution to one's personal library. By using the metaphor of a river and how it can provide you with both smooth sailing and dangerous white water, he captures numerous reminders that how we travel on this river is completely our choice.

He also reminds us that we are not alone and that we have support structures in our faith, in history and in the people around us to help us navigate the possible treacherous waters. This book is definitely an important read for anyone who wants to live a more empowered life; especially at this time as we all try to survive the changes we are facing, adapt to those changes, and ultimately flourish in our ability to succeed.

- **Mike Callahan**, Co-Owner, Callahan and Rose Consulting

The book you hold in your hands will be a compass for you in a time of great disruption. *Navigating Life's Journey: Common Sense in Uncommon Times* is written to spur the reader on to go deeper and think wider about the journey of life, even when that journey takes unexpected turns. As with his other books, Richard Battle writes of daily wisdom borne of thoughtful experience. The essays included here will help you not only find a way forward in rough waters they will also help you to embrace the joy that comes when you find the harbor. Take time to savor each essay and learn from the lessons insights that are offered. Your life will be enhanced by the experience!

– **Larry Coulter, Senior Pastor, The Lakeway Church**

Building on the foundations established in *Conquering Life's Course: Common Sense in Chaotic Times*, award-winning author Richard V. Battle returns with another collection of stories and inspirational messages designed to help readers uncover their inner strengths and follow their dreams.

The timing of this latest volume—written and published during the coronavirus pandemic, adds an element of urgency and perspective. In a world upended by crisis, there is no better time to begin the process of self-evaluation; to break down the barriers that are preventing us from realizing our potential, and to seek the happiness and purpose that God wants for each of us.

Battle's tone is folksy, friendly, and always encouraging. In example after example, he uses personal anecdotes and lessons from history to provide the nudge one needs to get off the bench and get into the game. As history has taught us (and Battle reminds us), we can't win if we don't try. And if the first attempt doesn't work, don't give up. Winners *never* quit.

Granted, fate deals us all different hands—but God never gives us more than we can handle. Once we acknowledge that, and the reality that many of life's obstacles are self-imposed, we can take responsibility for dismantling them and moving forward.

"It's never too late to start, and always too soon to give up!"

If you're not living your dreams, the first step to change is an easy one: Pick up a copy of *Navigating Life's Journey* and open yourself to the life you deserve.

- Gib Kearney, author of ***Reagan's Third Term***

Reminiscent of Benjamin Franklin, Richard Battle is a master at weaving stories with wisdom, humor, and real-life experiences. Each story is a meaningful life lesson on its own. When combined, these stories serve as a powerful guidebook for achieving our life's purpose without taking ourselves too seriously.

- **Susan L. Franzen** - Managing Partner, Pattern*Shifts*, LLC

Listen, I am not a person who revels in authority or tradition. I sometimes beat myself up over it because I know there is wisdom in the life and times of others. I know history and others' past experience and knowledge can save us from a lot of "pain". This book woke me up and helped me see a better way.

This is not only about Richard's insights. These are tried and true methods of many successful leaders. Being an Executive Coach and owning a business, Richard has shown real examples and tools in every chapter that will significantly increase your chances for success. If a person follows Richards' advice not only will they have better careers in business, they will have more fulfilled lives.

It's a shame that some will pass it by and not try the exercises and practices Richard suggests we all live by.

- **Michael W. Kublin - President PeopleTek Coaching and Consulting**

An eloquent and expansive look at our era, *Navigating Life's Journey* teaches this and future generations the value of discernment and why individuals must be able to know and express their "why" to others. We must look to our past for perspective, our present for connection, and our future for optimism so we can 'Aim High! Work Hard! And Never Quit!'

- Jennifer Heard, MBA, Professional Organizer, and Coach

A perfect combination of inspiration and information. In a year, where so many seem to have lost their way and have been overcome with fear, Richard shares his experience and knowledge on how we can keep faith, courage and restore core values

- Char Westfall, author of *A Beautiful Tragedy: A Navy SEAL Widow's Permission to Grieve and a Prescription for Hope*

Navigating Life's Journey is truly a game-changer! Richard V. Battle will inspire you to pursue your dreams through adventures that motivate, encourage, and challenge you to live life with purpose. It is a must-read for anyone who feels uncertain about the future and aspires to make a positive change. *Navigating Life's Journey* will steer you through all stages of your life with real tools that guide you on your journey toward success and happiness.

- Gayle Randall, Sr. Instructor of Management and Marketing, Angelo State University

ALSO BY RICHARD V. BATTLE

Conquering Life's Course – Common Sense in Chaotic Times

Unwelcome Opportunity – Overcoming Life's Greatest Challenges

Surviving Grief by God's Grace

The Volunteer Handbook – How to Organize and Manage A Successful Organization

The Four-Letter Word That Builds Character

The Master's Sales Secrets

NAVIGATING LIFE'S JOURNEY

*Common Sense in
Uncommon Times*

NAVIGATING LIFE'S JOURNEY

*Common Sense in
Uncommon Times*

RICHARD V. BATTLE

Outskirts Press, Inc.
http://www.outskirtspress.com

ISBN: 978-1-9772-3093-5

Copyright Registration Number/Date: TXu 2-213-814

Library of Congress Control Number: 2020912783

Cover Photo © 2021 Alamy.com. All rights reserved - used with permission.

Outskirts Press and the "OP" logo are trademarks belonging to Outskirts Press, Inc.

PRINTED IN THE UNITED STATES OF AMERICA

Dedication

In honor of my parents, grandparents, great grand-parents, and ancestors who went on before me, I dedicate this work with the hope of benefiting the lives of others.

I stand on your shoulders and those of everyone who contributed to my life. You share in any contribution that I might provide anyone.

TABLE OF CONTENTS

FOREWORD

The St. Joseph River rambles through 200 miles of towns and villages before casting its collective memories and meanderings into the easy waves of Lake Michigan just above the Indiana border. With its symphony of switchbacks, it clangs and clambers in a constant fight with the landscape before quietly surrendering to the big lake.

The "St. Joe" has been the source of life for human beings for millennia, before Michigan and Indiana were states, before the United States was a country, even thousands of years before generations of Miami tribes waded through its grey waters. In modern times, its freshwater flows from thousands of faucets and fleets of kayaks are found in the spaces where rapids have been tamed by the marriage of natural barriers and human engineering.

However, the river is impervious to the faces of the people and the names of the villages sharing in its generosity...and in its occasional fury. With time on its side, the river has seen names and faces come and go. For the people along its banks, these changes define history, and history is their story. For the St. Joe, all the stories flow into one.

Sometimes the St. Joe names one of its own. An example is South Bend, Indiana, broadly recognized as the home of the University of Notre Dame. South Bend is in the *northern* part of Indiana but sits on the *south bend* of the St. Joseph River, where the river sets its sights to the north and back to its motherland.

As a native (and proud) Texan, Richard Battle would not be the first person chosen to identify South Bend, or the "south bend," on a map of the United States. But Richard 'knows' the river. He knows the small towns and the villages. He knows the names.

In *Navigating Life's Journey*, the second book of Richard's series of short stories offering a unique perspective on managing the trials of life, Richard stands on the log raft, pole in hand, guiding our way. His stories are the towns and the villages. The names are his, but they are ours too.

Richard's stories illustrate the power of resiliency, faith, thankfulness, attitude, and action. He introduces us to the people and places responsible for his personal development and his spiritual growth.

Through his stories, Richard challenges us to be better. He uses the power of prose to point out the power within us to overcome personal setbacks. On the raft with Richard, we are at the river's mercy as we bounce off the banks and dodge debris, but through it all, we feel safe. We understand the underlying motivation is love.

Love exists in all. It flows through all. It flows into us and out from us. It never stops yet it can sometimes pool in places where it's most needed. Sometimes it's the St. Joe; sometimes is the Big Lake. It's where people gather and it gives people a reason to gather.

This is the central message from Richard. He believes in love. Even when in the toughest life lessons, love elbows its way in. Like the St. Joe, he challenges us to pass along these life lessons, rooted in love, to those around us, in our towns and villages, to honor our forbearers by returning their favor and passing the lessons forward to the next generation.

C. Steven Hartman
CEO, Alpha Kappa Psi Professional Business Fraternity

PREFACE

I write this during the 2020 COVID-19 (Corona Virus) worldwide pandemic. We know it will end, but we don't know when, how, or its impact on any of us personally.

Many people around the globe are suffering economically, emotionally, mentally, and physically. Large numbers of those experiencing this unique challenge have not had the opportunity to be tested in their lives before this event.

There is a stark difference in the attitude of people who are older and have experienced the ups and downs in life compared to the younger, less-experienced generations.

I think of my parents, grandparents, and others who lived through the depression of the 1930s and were immediately thrust into World War II. They grew up quickly because they had no time for frivolity. Life was hard every day, and nothing, including the largest governments, could erase the pain and suffering they endured for many years.

They were tough without being mean, serious without losing their sense of humor, prudent without being stingy, efficient with their time without sacrificing service to their fellow man, confident because they knew there was no benefit in worry, and faithful because they trusted their creator's eternal protection. They also knew there was nothing on this earth that could harm them permanently.

More times than I paid attention, they told stories of their experiences and the lessons that made indelible impacts on their entire lives. I'm sure they were disappointed their foresight and advice about financial prudence, keeping close with family, and holding onto to God at all costs seemed to fall on deaf ears.

Many times, Bill Battle, my dad, would exclaim, "This will work well unless everything goes into the sh@t#r." I'm sure there are many people, as I write this, that believe we are either there or rapidly heading there.

I believe our country, The United States, is better than that. Regardless of the depth, breadth, or length of this challenge, our people will overcome their pain and loss, and achieve new heights of success.

Despite many failures, our country was established on the twin principles of individual liberty endowed by our creator and free enterprise, enabling anyone to dream as big as they like and pursue their dream relentlessly. Our democracy marked the first time in history where each citizen has an equal voice, each state is represented equally, and those in any level of government serve the people. The rights of citizenship come with the equal counterbalance of responsibility. Too often, people insist upon their rights, but fewer stand tall carrying their share of the duty to their fellow citizens.

Benjamin Franklin, when asked what type of government he had given us at the Constitutional Convention in Philadelphia in September 1787, said, **"A republic if you can keep it."**

My late friend, mentor, and Texas Attorney General and Secretary of State, John Ben Shepperd, added emphasis to Franklin's inspiration stating, **"To be born free is an accident. To live free is a responsibility. But, to die free is an obligation."**

We stand on the shoulders of the founders, our ancestors, and others who went before us that gave us this republic we enjoy. Their hard work and sacrifice weren't only for their benefit, but to make the lives of their children and descendants easier than the ones they experienced.

We must broaden our shoulders by living responsible lives, caring for our families and neighbors. We should be good citizens and examples to our children and descendants, so they can stand on our shoulders. Doing so will prepare them to live successfully and develop their broad shoulders for future generations to stand on.

This volume is a humble contribution to the endeavors to sustain and enhance people's lives today and in the future. It continues the effort initiated in *Conquering Life's Course – Common Sense in Chaotic Times* by presenting ideas and principles celebrating traditional values from Western Civilization. I share my personal experiences and supplement them with stories and examples that are worthy of emulation.

Common Sense is always in season and NEVER goes out of style.

INTRODUCTION

This follow-up work to **Conquering Life's Course** is another collection of essays and stories commenting on the journey of life.

Each one celebrates common sense and is presented independently and tied together in this volume extolling age-old values proven through experience.

I present each subject with my personal experiences, examples of others, motivational quotes, and thought-provoking questions. My hope is for you to know my heart and the aspiration to share my life experiences to make the journey for others more fulfilling.

We have necessities and entitlements our parents could only dream about, and our grandparents couldn't conceive. We have to guard against our luxuries and leisure time, leading us to discard the gifts we have received. Thomas Sowell said, "Much of the social history of the western world, over the past three decades, has been a history of replacing what worked for what has sounded good." The opportunity and incentives offered by the free enterprise system propel our economy. Abandoning economic freedom for the disincentives of equality would destroy the energy of our economy and lead to mental, spiritual and financial stagnation.

I have chosen to utilize a river as a metaphor to illustrate the exploration of life. Rivers travel in many different forms. They vary in width, elevation and speed of current for example. From their source to their final destination, they move in the same way as our life's run from birth to death.

Rivers seem to flow endlessly. They exist today but have altered their form over time, just as the character of our society. The foundation of our values remains strong, and our edges are continually adapting like the banks of a river. Wind, rain, and erosion work on rivers to transform them just as social norms evolve.

Just as in life, rivers change quickly. They can go from quiet to flowing smoothly to unseen bends leading to roaring rapids and waterfalls as they travel in a seemingly unending procession to their end in a safe harbor or the sea. The uncertainty of what is unseen beyond today is one of the few certainties in life. I will stop in each of those areas of the river with life stories illustrating those characteristics.

As I have said before, the values I promote have been proven successful by time, our forefathers, and others who went before us. They built the most prosperous country in the history of the world. The norms of our civilization are still worthy of implementing as our bedrock providing us the sure footing and stability to modify the margins.

My sincerest desire is that you will be entertained, informed, and stimulated to think about your upbringing, beliefs, and plans to enrich your life. May your journey be dauntless, and you return the favor to those following behind us so that their travel will be even more successful and gratifying.

As you begin your journey, I hope the following Scripture will comfort you. **Isaiah 43:2** - When you pass through the waters, I will be with you; and when you pass through the rivers, they will not sweep over you.

Whatever you do

Aim High!
Work Hard!
Never Quit!

COVER PHOTO STORY

The picture chosen for the cover was deliberate and designed to utilize the metaphor of traveling the course of a river for living one's life.

I wanted to convey the majesty and beauty of life as displayed by the clear sky, mountains, evergreen trees, and smooth water.

Whether we're navigating the river or living our daily lives, if we employ the common sense proven over the ages in every situation we will make the journey more successful and enjoyable.

The man in the image represents each of us as we proceed through our lives. We pass each minute individually, but at various times our progress interacts with family, friends, co-workers, and others.

Our creator endows us with gifts, and the accumulation of our life experience helps make our trip smoother. If we're fortunate, we receive gifts from others that also enrich our lives.

I have acknowledged before that others have blessed me immensely. Some were known and others unknown to me in my life, and I stand on their shoulders.

My mission now is to provide timeless messages of proven principles to help people win every day.

Navigating Life's Journey and my other efforts aim to broaden my shoulders with the desire that others, today and in the future, may stand upon them.

My hope is you will see more beauty, peace, and enrichment in your life after reading the ideas I convey within these pages.

ACKNOWLEDGMENTS

I'm so grateful to my family for their continued support, assistance, and commitment. They have stood by me through success and failure, trial, and triumph. Thank you especially to my daughter Elizabeth, and brother Jerry and sister-in-law Cheryl Battle.

Words are insufficient to profess my appreciation for this volume and associated projects without the extraordinarily significant counsel and feedback of my long-time friend, mentor, and pastor Dr. Logan Cummings.

Thank you to my long-time friend and CEO of Alpha Kappa Psi Professional Business Fraternity, Steve Hartman, for contributing the Foreword to this volume and his encouragement of my endeavors.

I've included stories from friends, which are superb examples of the principles advocated in these pages. Thank you to Claudia Tangerife Castillo, Joe DeRossi, Jenine Lori, Dr. George Lowe, and Dan Marcinek for allowing me to share your achievements with my readers.

I appreciate the positive comments and encouragement for this project from Sam Chase, Joyce Christian, Doyle Gallman, C.B. Huchingson, Rick Rhodes, and John Smith.

Thank you to Burke Allen Adkins and Shaili Priya at Allen Media Strategies for their contributions to this volume and my speaking endeavors.

I appreciate Alane Pearce's consultation and editing of the manuscript. Her suggestions were invaluable.

Thank you to the team at Outskirts Press, including TinaMarie Ruvalcaba and Lisa Jones, for their assistance in bringing this project to life.

SECTION ONE
SMOOTH SAILING

Enthusiasm and Adventure

It Is NEVER Too Soon to Pursue Your Dreams

What are you and I waiting for to pursue our dream(s)?

Yes, I am as guilty as anyone as I deferred my dreams while responsibly providing a living for my family.

It doesn't have to be an all or nothing choice.

One of the great benefits of attending the 2019 Readers Favorite award ceremony for my book, *Unwelcome Opportunity,* was meeting authors from all over the world whose creativity and ideas inspired me.

The youngest winner was **Ellie Collins**, who at 13 years old was already twice published, and was there to receive her Honorable Mention award for *Mylee in the Mirror*. She won a silver award previously for ***Daisy, Bold and Beautiful***. She recently completed her third book.

Ellie is an extremely bright young lady who is involved in many normal activities for those her age and is also diligently pursuing her dreams as an author. It was refreshing speaking with her about her experiences, achievements, and vision.

She does not permit the, "**If only I were older**" fear to dissuade her pursuit of the life she wants to create for herself.

Too often, we hesitate or stop dead in our tracks because the most important two-letter word in the dictionary shows up in its most negative version. That word is **IF**.

The Merriam-Webster on-line dictionary tells us the word "if" is used as a condition or stipulation as a noun, and as to whether or not, as a conjunction. This formal definition is good, but it interests me how often it negatively limits our optimism and pursuit of our dreams.

A few examples of those limiting expressions include:

My life would be better today **If Only**?

I had more help.
I had more money.
I was younger.
I was older.
I knew more.
I was better looking.
I had more talent.
I was stronger.
I was faster.
I was bigger or smaller.
I was taller or shorter.
I was treated fairly.

Nearly everyone on the planet knows **Michael Dell**'s story of success, but how many people realize the number of challenges he overcame to build, grow, and continue to succeed with his business?

Before he became famous in the computer industry, he was a successful youth selling subscriptions to the *Houston Post* newspaper. Then, in his dorm room as a freshman at The University of Texas at Austin in 1984, he started a business selling upgrade kits for computers. From there, PC's Limited was born, which soon became Dell Computer, one of the world's largest technology companies.

Michael Dell's long-term success in an ever-changing business and economic environment is a testament to a leader who used IF in innovative ways instead of seeing it in a limiting light.

I believe most successful people avoid or ignore the word "if" when pursuing their dreams. They focus like Ellie Collins and Michael Dell on what steps they have to accomplish to succeed, and they relentlessly work to overcome any challenge to achieve their goals.

We need to surround ourselves with people who will encourage us in our efforts and avoid those people who add fear, uncertainty, and doubt into our thinking. Albert Einstein's advice is as accurate today as when he offered it. "Stay away from negative people. They have a problem for every solution." It worked well for him, and it will work well for us also.

Another successful person worth emulating is Theodore Roosevelt, former President of the United States. When troops complained about not having what they needed in Cuba during the Spanish-American War in 1898, Roosevelt told them, "Do what you can, with what you have, where you are at." We can't control our surrounding environment as we traverse the path to our success, but we can control how we respond, adapt, and overcome all challenges!

The next time you think you could do something If only, remember every great achiever overcame all of their "if" moments.

You Did What?

Have you ever reunited with friends after a long separation and been flabbergasted by their accomplishments?

We all establish definitions in our minds of the people we encounter in our lives. It is based primarily on our direct experiences with the individual and their reputation. We may pigeonhole others based on our perception of them and or be pigeonholed ourselves by other people's portrait of us.

Some people live their lives within that definition, and others amaze us with accomplishments far beyond our wildest imaginations.

We also have the opportunity to live our lives within narrow ranges of action, or continually push the limits of our capabilities and astound others.

There is no right way or one single best way to live. Thankfully, we have the freedom to choose how we navigate life's journey, and we can redefine our path multiple times during our lifetime.

An example of this phenomenon occurred when I attended my high school class reunion. I had recently published my fifth book and was discussing it with a classmate.

I stated that my former English teachers would be astonished to learn that I had read a book, much less written one. Proficiency in English was a stranger to me in high school and beyond. I never dreamed of writing one book much less more than one. My classmate concurred with my assessment, which we both laughed about, but I thought it might have a double meaning.

It dawned on me; I had accomplished more than I had dreamed in high school and college. While I had worked diligently over several years, I did not measure my progress against a past standard.

In my case at least, not thinking about my past dreams or a baseline was good because it gave me the liberty to fail and succeed in many efforts without contrasting them to a starting point.

RICHARD V. BATTLE

Who would have ever thought Fred LaNovel would live to be 102 years old, much less achieve everything he did? And although he is not well known, his life is worth learning about.

I was introduced to him in 1986 through an article in *The Austin American Statesman* on July 24th. He began in the family business, which was an aerial act in the circus, but he didn't allow his beginning to define him.

He flew an airplane before World War I, served in the United States Navy during the war, took up painting after his 90th birthday, and he learned to walk again on artificial legs when he was 98 years old after he lost his legs due to a circulatory disease. He always strove to finish what he started.

Fred LaNovel's philosophy of life has inspired me since reading the article. **"To achieve all that is possible, we must attempt the impossible. To be as much as we can be, we must dream of being more."** I believe Fred's zest to continue learning, strive, and complete ever-growing dreams enabled him to live an extraordinarily adventuresome and long life.

What will you regret if you don't attempt it in your lifetime? Isn't falling short of a dream better than regret? Isn't it possible you might achieve something beyond your wildest imagination? You never know what you might accomplish.

WHAT'S MY DREAM?

What great goal would you attempt if you thought there was a possibility of achieving it?

The expression "Life is tough," is well worn and trite, but also very true. As we traverse life's course, it reinforces its truth.

Another saying is also true, and I have survived long enough to testify to its authenticity: "That which doesn't kill you will make you stronger."

I'm blessed to have experienced more successes than I have deserved in life, and more failures and challenges than I desired. Most of us experience a course in life that is more demanding than we would choose for ourselves.

Our opportunity to grow is in how we respond to failure. Do we cease our attempts to reach ever higher in fulfilling our life's mission, or do we pick ourselves up and continue our quest to be the best person we can be?

I'm a better person because of the lessons learned from my experiences where I fell short of success. While it is beneficial to learn from our own experiences, we often can learn so much more from the inspiration we receive from others' lives.

I first learned about Paul Alexander in a 1986 *Austin American Statesman* article about him passing the bar exam to practice law in Texas. He had graduated from the University of Texas Law School in 1984. Becoming a lawyer at 40 was mildly unique, but the other obstacle he overcame should encourage all of us to attempt dreams otherwise thought impossible.

As a child in the 1950s, Paul contracted Polio. It is a disease that attacked primarily young children's muscles and could result in paralysis and even death. Parents were frightful their children would contract this highly contagious disease. They were grateful in 1955 when Dr. Jonas Salk invented the vaccine, practically eradicating the disease in the United States.

Paul was compelled at six-years-old to live in an "iron lung" because he was not only paralyzed, he couldn't breathe on his own. The iron lung is a large, horizontal metal tube the patient lays in with only his or her head protruding from the open end. It enables the patient to breathe more regularly and easily.

RICHARD V. BATTLE

Paul could have lain in the machine and used it as an excuse to freeze his life's achievements and impact, but that wasn't the choice he made. Holding a rubber-tipped stick between his teeth, Paul would turn the pages of his schoolbooks. He writes by holding a pen in the same way. He has helpers prepare his work for him.

Utilizing this technique, Paul graduated second in his high school class in Dallas and from SMU. He was determined to become a lawyer and fulfilled his dream in 1986.

In 2018, a *Dallas Morning News* article updated Paul's story. He is now a semi-retired bankruptcy attorney. His parents gave him the character and motivation to achieve far more than anyone dreamed possible for him. They taught him, ***The most important thing is faith in self and faith in God. Anything you can dream will come true.***

When I think about a daunting opportunity and how easy it would be to not attempt it, I'm reminded of Paul Alexander. I have achieved more than I thought possible, and even if a failure, I have achieved far more than I would if I had not dared to attempt the endeavor.

What's one great thing you would like to achieve? Would you rather live with the regret of not attempting it or the failure of not achieving it? Who knows, you may succeed beyond your wildest imagination!

Why President Ronald Reagan's Leadership is Worth Emulating

As we grow and develop our leadership skills, it is a worthy exercise to study successful leaders for lessons that can contribute to our efforts. Who are the leaders you look up to and why? I submit President Ronald Reagan is more than worthy for several reasons. Below are only a very few examples of them.

He was elected president at an age when most people slowed down and enjoyed retirement. President Reagan demonstrated it is NEVER Too Late to positively impact others.

On March 30, 1981, I was in Caracas Venezuela on a company rewards trip. When we returned to the cruise ship that afternoon, I vividly remember listening to the British Broadcasting Corporation (BBC) report on the assassination attempt on our president. Little did we know how close he came to losing his life that day.

I couldn't imagine then I would have the privilege to see him speak in San Antonio. It was his first public speech after the attempted assassination at The United States Junior Chamber of Commerce national convention. My friends and I were relegated to the cheap seats in the Hemisfair Arena. President Reagan's voice was weak that day, and we strained to hear his every word. I'll never forget the goosebumps I experienced when he closed with the inspiration for our civic group to give more to our fellow citizens.

"If not you, who? If not now, when?" he inquired. You could feel the energy from the thousands of people in the hall who were ready to storm out and give of themselves because our beloved president asked us to do so. President Reagan's positive attitude was contagious and lifted the United States out of the malaise of the 1970s.

Below is an excerpt from *The Four-Letter Word that Builds Character* I wrote in 2006 celebrating his positive outlook on life.

Ronald Reagan was an unlikely person to be elected President of the United States. A radio broadcaster and actor, he was first elected as Governor of California in his fifties.

As an elected official, Reagan had those who agreed and disagreed with his political views. However, he was beloved by the people because of his positive attitude and approach toward life. He related to every man, and almost every man related to him. "His real heroes were common folk who performed uncommon feats of self-denial and courage."[1]

As President, Reagan had a vision of where he wanted to lead the country, the principles to stay focused on the course to achieve his objectives, and the positive outlook to persevere despite opposition and reversals. He brought dignity to the presidency and the country after a tumultuous period.

One of his greatest legacies was instituting policies eventually ending the Cold War. President Reagan pursued bold initiatives with conviction while some doubted his competence.

His willingness to walk away from negotiations with the Soviets at their summit meeting in Reykjavik, Iceland in 1986 demonstrated his style of negotiating from confidence and strength rather than fear. The resulting paradigm, shift when combined with other strategies, culminated with the Berlin Wall falling in 1989 and the collapse of the Soviet Union in 1991. The Cold War was won without firing a shot, and President Reagan made a significant contribution to the victory.

Known as the great communicator, Reagan was unparalleled at his use of humor. His jokes entertained people and helped them to better understand his message. He often poked fun at himself, which helped people to relate to him.

Reagan was self-assured, and more importantly, he was confident in the ability of others. His optimism inspired people to be more than they were, and his example demonstrated the possibility to achieve one's dreams. The resulting pride in America and being American resulted in a period of peace and prosperity. President Reagan's positive attitude and leadership were as important as any policy in the positive impact produced by his presidency.

We stand on the shoulders of those who went before us. We benefit from their lives and examples. What kind of shoulders will we provide to those who come behind us? I hope we don't let them down.

This chapter was first published in *The Washington Examiner* on February 5th, 2020 as an opinion article.

THE NEW THREE R'S
OF SUCCESS

Remember *the three R's* and how mastering them meant you were educated properly? What are the new three R's today that will ensure you will succeed in your every endeavor?

In their original contextual slang, the three R's are reading, writing and arithmetic (reading, 'rigting and 'rithmetic). I would submit in addition to those, there are three new R's today that are essential to success.

The first R of success is **resilience in failure**. It is easy to miss early failings in successful people because those individuals often don't show up on our radar until they burst onto the scene with their "overnight" success. People admire and focus on the achievement, but often overlook the trials and defeats proceeding it.

You may be surprised to learn Bill Gates, Steven Spielberg, J.K. Rowling, and Steve Jobs failed before their mega-success. Other examples of people who failed before success include the often more familiar names of Albert Einstein and Abraham Lincoln.

I want to submit one other name that may surprise you. When you visit Disneyland or Disney World, see a child with the black mouse ears, or see a movie with the iconic castle logo at the end, do you know they are the result of one man's refusal to quit?

Would you believe **Walt Disney** was a school dropout, was rejected by the army because he was too young, failed in his first business venture, and was terminated by a newspaper because he wasn't creative enough?

Disney recognized the lessons of failure as he persevered in the quest for his dreams. He said, "All the adversity I've had in my life, all my troubles and obstacles, have strengthened me… You may not realize it when it happens, but a kick in the teeth may be the best thing in the world for you."

His tenacity led to his creating one of the most successful family entertainment empires of all time. His success was present in his cartoons, movies, television, and theme parks, and continues to thrive and benefit millions of people more than fifty years after his death.

The second R of success is being **resourceful in ideas**. Too often, people are wedded to a narrow range of thought when attempting a great enterprise. After exhausting all of the possibilities they can devise, they cease their effort.

Nearly everyone knows **Orville and Wilbur Wright** for inventing and soaring in the first manned motorized flying machine on December 17, 1903. What few know is the winding path leading to their invention and immortality.

Although they were industrious, no one could have imagined where the journey of their lives would lead. After, opening a bicycle shop in Dayton, Ohio, a dream to do more and be more settled upon them.

They became fascinated with the idea of building a flying machine. Neither had a formal engineering education. They learned as they proceeded. Unlike others around the world working on the same goal, they never sought nor received any government subsidies, but self-funded the venture.

After initially building, flying, and failing with their first design of a glider, they redesigned the plane and repeated the process with their next glider design. Progress occurred, but additional setbacks limited their success.

However, their dream was not to build a glider, but a flying machine powered by an engine. Their mechanic, Charles Taylor, built an engine because the requisite one that met the requirements demanded was unavailable.

Again, failures and weather challenges continued to thwart their efforts. They persisted, willingly adjusted their design, and eventually made history.

The December 17, 1903 flight was not the culmination of the Wright brother's efforts, but a milestone on the way to further successes. Wilbur Wright said, "A man who works for the immediate present and its immediate rewards is nothing but a fool."

Once the Wright brothers unleashed man from gravity by a flying machine, future development advanced at a rapid rate. My grandparent's lives spanned from before the Wright brother's success and after the July 16, 1969 moon landing of Apollo 11. They saw the impossible that Etienne-Jules Marey asked about, "How many intentions have we seen realized which have been pronounced impossible?"

The third R of success is being **relentless in the pursuit of your dreams.** We see many successful people through the lens that the field of their triumph is the only area of expertise they have endeavored to achieve. So often, people who fail in one area warehouse the lessons they learned from the reversal. They then assimilate a wide variety of ideas at one time in another venture that is wildly successful.

Mark Cuban is one of the untold number of examples. Before his success as the owner of The Dallas Mavericks and appearing on the television show *Shark Tank,* he failed in a string of efforts. Cuban sold garbage bags, ran newspapers, and fell short as a bartender a short-order cook, and a computer salesman.

He eventually began and then sold his own software company, and then repeated the success with broadcast.com. Cuban's achievements were the culmination of all of his previous shortfalls and served as the springboard to further accomplishments with the Mavericks and *Shark Tank*.

Not one to rest on his laurels, Cuban continues to expand his fields of influence and triumphs with contributions to the discussions in politics and current events. He epitomizes as Winston Churchill said, "Success is not final; failure is not fatal: it is the courage to continue that counts."

In addition to securing a broad formal education, including the traditional 3 R's of reading, writing, and arithmetic, we must excel in the new 3 R's of success for today and tomorrow.

The 3 New R's of Success today are:

Resilience in failure.

Resourceful in identifying and adopting new ideas.

Relentless pursuit of your dream.

What great dream do you have you can achieve if you're resilient, resourceful, and relentless? Who can help you with the effort? Where can you secure the necessary resources to end your journey successfully?

Become the You You're Meant to Be

Are you on the course of your life journey you planned, or are you meandering along unaware of where you'll end up? Are you satisfied with your current position? Do you have unfulfilled dreams?

Day-to-day living has extinguished the dreams of more people than virtually any other obstacle. Whether we begin our journey with a grand vision or develop one over time, many abandon their efforts along the way.

Our final destination in life is not the result of any individual decision. We contribute to a successful life choice-by-choice.

We can also ruin our reputation and significantly set back our efforts with a single misstep.

Those who succeed over a lifetime make daily choices that propel them forward while others choose to play and ignore the future. One example of this is how people handle their finances.

Some people set aside money for a rainy day regardless of how much or how little they have. When the storm arrives, their preparation enables them to endure it with less stress and long-term damage. Other people spend more than they make despite fair warnings of potential storms. When the same storm appears, they are woefully unprepared and suffer short-and-long-term catastrophe.

In our youth, we perceive life as an endless adventure. It is easy to disregard how we want to be viewed at its end, and the result is often decisions based on short-term gratification that have no long-term merit. We should NEVER let today become more important than eternity!

I strongly believe we begin every day on a threshold. As I wrote in *The Four-Letter Word that Builds Character*, "What you do in the present, will create a past, that will greatly influence your opportunities and dreams in the future." It is our choice daily and I have not and will never be perfect.

Even if we begin life with a grand quest, we will inevitably face trials and tribulations. A long life will usually include several, and again our choices will define how they impact our journey.

I agree with the late novelist, James Lane Allen, who said, "Adversity doesn't build character, it reveals it." When we're tested, what is inside us, including the lessons from past challenges, is unveiled by our response to the hardship. Facing difficulties does build endurance and resilience, which increases our confidence to absorb the next threat we encounter. My late friend, Lewis Timberlake, said it another way; "When the storm clouds come, the eagle flies and the small birds run for cover."

It is imperative for us to relentlessly continue our path regardless of the degree of difficulty until our last breath! One must merely look at the difference made by Winston Churchill's determination upon ascending to the office of Prime Minister in England in May of 1940. Germany appeared invincible and was all but certain to invade their island at any moment. Several members of his cabinet encouraged him to negotiate a peaceful surrender.

Undeterred, Churchill told a stunned House of Commons on June 4, 1940, that England would fight Germany and would **NEVER surrender**. His attitude and resolve galvanized the British people and laid the foundation for the allies winning World War II.

I learned the hard way it isn't important how long our journey is in days or years. My mentor and former pastor, Dr. Logan Cummings, taught me this during his funeral service for my son John who passed away suddenly and unexpectedly at nine-months of age. Dr. Cummings said, "The impact of a life is more important than its length." This lesson, and others that I have shared since his passing, have positively impacted more people than he may have otherwise. While I still grieve where he isn't, I'm grateful his life has had such a significant impact.

Along our journey, many people known and unknown who went before us provided assistance to ease our way. Regardless of our decisions and choices, we wouldn't be as far down the stream without their contributions. We stand on their broad shoulders and need to broaden our shoulders so the next generations can stand on them. I prefer to say we should **Return the Favor** of our predecessors' gifts to others to achieve that end.

Finally, for those of us who believe in a Creator, we must recognize that who we are and the gifts that we have been given are from God. Similar to presents given by our family and friends, how will God feel if we break or waste the gifts He has given us? If we cherish and utilize our gifts positively and for the benefit for others, might we receive more opportunities and responsibilities?

What we become and the impact that we make on others with what we have been given is our gift back to God. We can never repay His blessings, but we can strive to maximize our favors in the effort to do so. We must finish our journey exhausted in the endeavor!

How Do You Become the Person That You're Meant to Be?

- **Make every decision based on how we want people to see us at the end of our life.**
- **Every day act differently than others to have what they won't have tomorrow.**
- **Don't let today become more important than eternity.**
- **NEVER quit or surrender regardless of the difficulties encountered.**
- **Remember that the impact of a life is more important than its length.**
- **RETURN the favor of the gifts you've been given.**
- **Understand that what you become is your gift to God.**

Our effort to achieve the perfect self we are meant to be is never completed. If we are faithful to pursue and persist in the attempt to accomplish our destiny, we will finish our journey in safe harbor.

I wish you safe travels on your life's journey, and that you end up far beyond the dreams you imagined.

Timing May Not Be Everything, but It Is the Essential Thing!

"Timing is everything" has been said often. If it isn't everything, it certainly is the essential thing in successful enterprises.

Can you remember great things you realized because of perfect timing? Can you also remember setbacks you suffered due to poor, premature or late timing?

This fact is nothing new, as countless examples stretch into Biblical times. Moses spent forty years in the desert being prepared by God to return to Egypt as the instrument to free the Jewish people from their captivity. Little David had to wait fourteen years to become king from the time God chose him until he ascended the throne in Israel. Was their waiting period a vacation? Certainly not. Moses and David grew and matured in wisdom and experience that enabled them to succeed in their respective missions.

Before I speak to successful examples due to good timing, let's look at two illustrations of loss or failure resulting from ill-timed actions. While there are too many real examples to choose from, a classic illustration from literature is well known.

The story of Romeo and Juliet is almost universally known and includes enough drama to qualify as a modern-day reality show. After more twists than a Formula One racetrack, Romeo finds Juliet apparently dead, but comatose in reality. Distraught due to his loss and the accumulation of drama, Romeo ingests poison to join his beloved in death.

Juliet awakes from her drug-induced coma to find Romeo dead and stabs herself to join him in death.

There isn't enough popcorn to ease the pain resulting from the loss of the cherished young lovers.

Substantially less well known, but significantly more painful (because it was very personal), was my life-lesson in rental real estate investing.

I was seven years into implementing a successful plan that would have led to financial independence. A decision of mine, and events beyond my control in 1986, crisscrossed and led to my economic destruction.

My choice to add a property to my portfolio was sound based on the conditions of the economy in late 1985. Little did I know, The Tax Reform Act of 1986 would turn investment equations for me, and thousands of others, upside down.

My monthly cash flow went from even to a negative $ 2,500 within ninety days of the law's passage. The new economics of those investments' increasing depreciation time negatively hammered property values by roughly thirty percent as people tried to unload their units. The result was that you couldn't give a property away, but I had to pour good dollars after bad ones.

Month-after-month the pain and stress continued as I watched my savings drained. It felt like my suffering would never end. Eventually my suffering did end, but not until I endured three years of agony.

This lesson on timing was extremely costly to me. I learned how things beyond one's control could ruin you, and real-life economics.

Thankfully, I have benefitted from timing either by my choice or good fortune, as well. As you can imagine, these examples are much more pleasant to share.

Benjamin Disraeli, former British prime minister, said, "One secret of success in life is for a man to be ready for his opportunity when it comes." How correct he was as I relate two personal experiences where my delay in action produced much better results than if I had proceeded earlier.

While in college, I was a member and chapter president of Alpha Kappa Psi professional business fraternity. As was common in those days, life after graduation was focused elsewhere. Long before the days of cell phones and the internet, it was easy to lose touch with my friends. I focused my civic activities in other areas and lost touch with the fraternity.

After a long absence, I reconnected with the organization to speak at a regional training event. That led me to serve four years on the chairman's advisory council, which further led me to serve nine years on the board of directors, including two as board chairman.

My experience was beyond fulfilling as it enriched my life beyond my expectation. As I reflected on the years away from the group, I didn't see them as lost, but as a time I prepared myself to enjoy and serve the organization. If I had continued my participation and service directly beyond my college experience, neither the organization nor I would have benefitted as much as when I was more mature and experienced.

When I graduated from college, I was dating a young lady who was the administrative assistant for the Austin Junior Chamber of Commerce (Jaycees). My father had been a Jaycee when I was younger, and I had a very favorable opinion of the organization. For whatever reason, I chose not to join the organization at that time. Little did I know how my delay would benefit me!

Seven years later, my softball teammate Matt Walker, spoke of his Jaycee involvement at one of our games. I told him I would like to join also and proceeded to do so at their next meeting. The experience was life-changing for me.

Besides, receiving major organization and individual national and international recognition, that experience led me to publish my first book, *The Volunteer Handbook: How to Organize and Manage a Successful Organization* in 1988. I never dreamed of writing one book, much less additional volumes resulting from the confidence gained from the first effort.

Looking back, I recognize I would not have gained the life-long friends, experienced the same success, personal and leadership growth, or impact if I had that membership experience at a younger age.

For us to maximize our readiness to succeed whenever the opportunity arrives, we can practice a few proven habits.

How We Can Prepare to Succeed When the Time Is Perfect?

- Go above and beyond your work requirements to learn and demonstrate your abilities.
- Be a life-long learner from the experience of yours and others.
- Proactively increase your education by reading, studying, and actively engaging in activities to broaden your capabilities.
- Invest your time and treasure for your future success.
- Learn the difference between patiently persisting in your actions and overexerting your ambitions. The first leads to long-term success and healthy relationships, and the second only rewards you materially in the short term.
- Be ready when the opportunity arrives to grasp it and confidently excel in it.

I'm sure you with a little time can cite your examples of good and bad timing.

The question for all of us is, will we exercise daily preparation to be ready when our opportunity comes?

If You Don't Know Where You're Going, You'll Get Where You Get

If our trip results in reaching an undesired location, whom will we hold responsible?

First, I admit my guilt in not following what I am advocating now during a large portion of my life. Despite my unplanned travel, I enjoyed success in many fields. Fortunately, through many rapids, dead end forks and detours, I arrived at an overlook where I could see my ultimate destination.

As I endeavor daily to progress toward my objective, I find my efforts more rewarding than I ever imagined. I hope these ideas will contribute to you see your destination more quickly and clearly to enable your trip to be more fulfilling.

Simplifying our life trip to three stages, we embark on our grand adventure when we're born, and our final destination is revealed upon our death. In between, we each travel a unique route in time, direction, length, and difficulty based on many things, but mostly on our choices as we progress.

Our embarkation is usually met with little fanfare, except by our family and their friends. While not apparent at the time, each day we absorb input from our parents and other sources that contribute from that point forward to our knowledge, decisions, and actions.

In the beginning, we are focused on the shortest-term necessities of nourishment and comfort. If we're not provided for on our timetable, everyone within earshot is alerted by our cries.

During childhood, our time horizon lengthens but is still much shorter than that of a mature adult. We focus on progressing from one school year to the next, worrying about others' perceptions of us, and other items that seem like life-and-death matters then, but are relegated to unimportant later.

Our life objectives are often vague and purposeless. If we are only focused on the short-term, our decisions will only be based on that view. If we don't mature and expand our horizon, where we end up will be less based on our choice than the life experiences that accumulate.

$$\sim\sim\sim$$

As we proceed on our unique route, we will begin to focus on longer-term decisions such as careers, life-partners, principles, and beliefs. While our advancement varies, most of us wish that we would have set our sights further into the future earlier; I know that I sure do.

Stephen Covey's **_The 7 Habits of Highly Effective People_** encourage us to think farther into the future. He advocates that there are two realities. The first is mental and the second one is the physical action executing what was visualized.

Covey's 1989 widely acclaimed volume has changed the lives of millions living today and those of future generations. It overflows with wisdom on living effectively.

He utilizes the metaphor of visualizing your reputation with others at your funeral service. What do we want others to think and say about us? We may not think individual daily decisions would impact the end of our life, but they do. It takes a lifetime to build a positive reputation, but one can be destroyed by one decision.

If we're thinking only about what we're doing this weekend, our decisions will reflect that thinking. On the other hand, the choices we make to earn the reputation we desire at the end of our life will inspire us to make each of them more thoughtfully and well-reasoned.

If we remain true to our principles and values, the course of our route will be smoother and we will travel farther toward our desired destination than if we are less faithful in our discipline.

Sometimes, we know what we would like to accomplish, but we don't know exactly where achieving that object will deposit us at the end of our life.

Many of you are familiar with the Lewis and Clark expedition. Its goal was to discover a cross-continent waterway between Missouri and the Pacific Ocean. The benefits of that achievement include increased commerce, securing more land for the United States, and scientific discoveries.

When the Corps of Discovery left in August of 1803, it was a true missionary exploration because no one knew if they would achieve their objectives, how long the trip would take, what they would encounter, or if they would even survive. Their courage, resourcefulness, resilience, and relentlessness were unsurpassed.

After traveling more than 8,000 miles, reaching the Pacific Ocean, interacting with many native Americans, receiving assistance from Sacagawea, discovering and documenting hundreds of scientific facts, and only losing one man; they returned to St. Louis in October of 1806.

While they achieved so much, they didn't find the all-water route to the Pacific; having a large target provided them focus and drive that resulted in them reaching the ocean.

Unfortunately, Lewis believed he failed in his mission, leading to his tragic and premature demise. President Jefferson and others felt otherwise, and we continue to benefit from their efforts.

Many other examples can be cited proving the principle **if you have a goal, you will achieve more even if you don't achieve your goal.**

Our ambition should be to learn and adopt proven principles of behavior, identify our life's purpose as early as possible, and specify and document our mission and goals.

When we know these things about ourselves, we can travel our route with clarity and confidence every day knowing that our final destination will reveal the person that we aspire others to see in us.

How Can We Revise Our Course to Reach our Desired Destination?

- **Recognize that not setting a course for a specific destination will result in losing control of where we arrive.**
- **Seek and find purpose in life, which will reveal our desired destination.**

- Live every decision and every day in support of traveling your identified route.
- If you experience a setback for whatever reason, don't quit or beat yourself up, but recommit to your goal, correct your course, refocus your effort, and be grateful you're back where you want to be.
- Enjoy the knowledge that whenever you arrive at your final destination you will be viewed as you desired. Many people will benefit along your way and beyond your lifetime from your contributions to our world.

May you discover your calling, redirect your route, enjoy the trip, and celebrate your successful arrival at the safe harbor you set out to reach.

Taking Advantage of the Wisdom of the Ages Before Your Time

What great dreams would you attempt if you knew you would succeed? How can you increase your odds of success and pursue your dreams earlier?

Western civilization developed on the backs of millions of people over hundreds of years. No, it isn't and will never be perfect. Despite the brokenness of this world, more charity, culture, and grace have resulted than with any society previously.

Until recently, each generation revered the benefits they inherited. They worked diligently by adding their imprint to improving society before they departed. They read and studied successes and failures, adding them to their education from others. Their endeavors provided solid foundations of wisdom to make deliberative decisions based on precedent, knowledge, and compassion.

Things have changed drastically! I ask, **"If hindsight is 20/20 and experience is the best teacher, why are young people who have neither, always so quick to ignore the experience available from those who have both?"**

Now we are in the midst of a cultural war where young people neither know nor care about the generations preceding them. They believe their superior intellect entitles them to throw away everything from history to remake the present for their collective convenience.

They are a cabal of destroyers who criticize imperfect people without care for their positive contributions. They have not, nor are they capable of building anything on their own. If left to their devices, they will crush all the gains made by previous generations and leave us with a dog-eat-dog anarchical society. They believe they can deliver a utopia that no group in history has succeeded in establishing to date.

What do we do?

~~

Depending on whether we are beginning life or nearing a safe harbor, our actions will vary. Regardless, recognizing the madness of throwing away everything generations lived-and-died to bequeath us is paramount for all.

While I will recommend steps for mature adults at the end of this chapter, I will focus primarily on thoughts to help young people succeed and live more fulfilling lives.

I often heard my dad quote Ben Franklin's sage advice, **"Life's tragedy is that we get old too soon and wise too late." No, I didn't appreciate its wisdom sufficiently, but I hope my alarm will alert you earlier in your life.**

NOW is your time to invest in yourself and your family as much and as early as possible. Consume the lessons of the ages instead of focusing on the pleasure of the moment.

Timeless truths benefiting you include:

- **Human nature doesn't change.** It's the same today as yesterday and every day before.
  - » Using half-truths as deception is as old as time itself. Adam and Eve were both deceived by the serpent in the Garden of Eden.
  - » They both blamed each other for their failure. People still shirk responsibility today.
- **Our culture promotes self, the present, and material things.**

- » They provide only momentary satisfaction and success.
- » Read Solomon's writings in Ecclesiastes in the Bible for proof.
- The key to long term success and happiness is:
  - » **Live for a lifetime and eternity.**
  - » **Live for relationships and the non-material things in life.**
- **Live for others and honor God.**
  - » **Serving the needs of others is gratifying and is commended by God.**
- **It's what you don't see that can get you in trouble.**
  - » Learn to read between the lines and verify everything.
- **What you see isn't always what you'll get.**
  - » **Life is full of mysteries. There are things seen that drive us crazy and things unseen that give us a peace we can entrust for our eternity.**
- **Patience is learned primarily from painful practice.**
  - » Make sure you learn from each setback so you don't suffer twice for one lesson.
- **If you can control your emotions, especially anger, you'll have fewer apologies to make.**

When I was a boy, my greatest days were spent on my grandparent's farm. We fished, hunted, explored, got into a lot of mischief, and occasionally helped with the chores.

As my younger brother, Jerry, and I traversed the property, he would often follow me through a gate I opened for us. Pressing on, I expected Jerry to close the gate and continue following me. Maybe he was an early-day protester, because he marched through the opening without as much as a pretense of shutting it.

Believing Jerry would be disciplined for not shutting it, I continued. I don't remember if or how many cows escaped the pasture; I do remember my surprise when I was punished and spanked soundly!

"Why am I in trouble since he was the last one through the gate?" I asked my dad.

"You're older, and you should have known better than to leave the gate open, even if he didn't close it," he replied.

I'm embarrassed to admit I didn't learn my lesson quickly enough in this case. The lightbulb finally went off at a later date, and the lesson soaked in. I wish I had asked more questions. This lesson is another example of the benefit of kids asking "why" so often.

This story illustrates that life is full of lessons. Instruction shows up in unexpected places sometimes. Some lessons come earlier than others, some come easier than others, and some hurt my bottom more than others.

My desire sharing this story is so it will provide you an example of serving more than a laugh at my ineptness.

Below are some specific ideas to serve others and enhance your life based on your position.

How Can Young People Benefit from the Life Experiences of Others?

- Recognize others hold the wisdom of the ages.
- Determine learning from others experience will expedite your success and enhance your life.
- Seek one or more mentors who care about you and are willing to share their knowledge with you.
- Be a life learner of history and the world from many sources.
- Encourage your peers in the value of your path.
- Lead, share, and inspire those coming behind you to follow in your footprints.

How Do We Use Our Experience to Impact the Future, Preserve its Best Parts, and Modify its Shortcomings?

- Recognize our destination will be the same as other failed societies without action.
- Determine the knowledge of our understanding.
- Identify the gifts we have been given to share our experiences.
- Share our expertise with those who will listen.
- Encourage like-minded others to do likewise.
- Be confident your gift to others will benefit many during and beyond your lifetime.

Yes, it is frustrating when we observe people who don't know or care to learn from the wisdom of the ages. But we can't abandon our efforts to help others based on the rejection of a few.

There is no way to know how many people our efforts will impact or over what time or level. We have to be satisfied with the fact that we acted to make a difference.

PRIVILEGED

Have you determined which privilege you should renounce because of your guilt yet? I am guilty of one privilege I refuse to surrender.

My mother used to tell me when I was young how fortunate I was to live in The United States. Like many children, I assumed I was entitled to what I had received, and most people around the globe lived similar lives. As I matured and traveled the world, my appreciation for my mother's teaching increased.

I'm thankful my formal education occurred before today's partisan brawls to influence curriculum's based on politics and vast sums of money because then, both major political parties agreed on the country's founding and its exceptional nature based on God's gift. Most people cherished The Declaration of Independence, The Constitution, the flag, our national anthem, and the benevolence we shared from our bounty toward other countries.

We now live in interesting times. Instead of focusing on what unites us and our shared contributions to build a "more perfect union" (as stated as the first objective in the Preamble of The United States Constitution), people divide into groups and attack others. Most of us never dreamed party politics would result in separating us from our defining principles. I have no doubt that there is much more that unites us than divides us.

Yes, we're privileged in how our founders prepared, deliberated, and declared independence based on ideals with logic and reason instead of the emotion found in the French revolution occurring shortly after our own.

Thirteen disparate colonies overcame their differences to unite against the tyranny of King George III of England. Fifty-six men risked not only their "lives, fortunes, and sacred honor" if the effort failed; they not only risked everything for liberty but suffered greatly to lay the foundation of our privilege.

Nine of our founding fathers died fighting or from hardship, twelve had their homes pillaged and destroyed by the British, five were captured and tortured before dying, two lost sons, another had two sons captured, and others lost wives and fortunes.

The war for our independence lasted seven years and cost about 25,000 lives—the lives of people who sacrificed but never breathed the air of liberty resulting from their gift to us.

The Articles of Confederation was the first government enacted after securing our freedom, but failed after a few years because the states were more united in name than function.

Our current Constitution was authored in 1787, but not without many disagreements and compromises. Slavery was codified to secure the necessary votes for passage, but for the first time, a republic securing rights for individuals and limiting the rights of government was legislated. Our gift of privilege as free citizens with the power and responsibility to restrict governments from enslaving us was delivered.

Benjamin Franklin knew the tendency for governments to enlarge their power at the expense of the individual. On exiting the hall after concluding the Constitution's creation, a woman asked him, "Dr. Franklin, what kind of government have you given us?" He replied, "A republic, if you can keep it."

Our forefathers after Franklin remained true to our founding principles and have bequeathed to us through additional sacrifice this unique gift no country was ever given.

For more than two hundred years, efforts were made at various speeds to make our union more perfect. About six hundred thousand died to end slavery in the Civil War, lasting four years. The vote was extended to women in 1920. The effort continues.

Like all worthy ideals, those enumerated in the Declaration of Independence are unachievable by imperfect human beings. It does not mean we should not relentlessly pursue them. We should celebrate progress toward their achievement, and learn from the shortcomings of our efforts.

Today, the politician's quest for power and the corrupting influence of money at all levels of society, but especially in public administration, have overwhelmed principle. Generations of freedom, wealth, and minimal sacrifice have resulted in people believing the price of freedom was paid forever. That attitude threatens our future and that of our children!

What should we do to terminate our current decline and resume our individual and national ascent?

How Do We Use our American Privilege to Repay the Gift?

- **Appreciate the gift of liberty we have been given.**
- **Recognize our country isn't a perfect one but is exceptional.**

- **Overcome the perception** we can't make a difference in improving the future; Sydney Smith said, "It is the greatest of all mistakes to do nothing when you can only do a little. Do what you can."
- **Determine where and how we can best contribute our efforts.**
- **Educate our children and grandchildren on the sacrifice of so many, resulting in our liberty.**
- **Remind others that freedom is bought one generation at a time, and it is our responsibility now.**
- **Encourage people to show up, stand up, and speak up to defend our gift against all who seek to destroy it for ideals that have never worked anywhere in the world.**

We stand on the shoulders of giants, though imperfect, whose gift to us will be in vain if we do not extend it to the next generations.

As my late friend, mentor, and Texas Attorney General and Secretary of State John Ben Shepperd said, **"To be born free is an accident. To live free is a responsibility. But, to die free is an obligation."** We who are citizens by birth, or by naturalization, should realize the accident that deposits us in a free land. Every day; internal and external, seen and unseen threats to our freedom pursue robbing us of our liberty.

Each of us will choose our actions to ensure breathing our last breath as a free person. None of us can assure our success in the effort, but if every one of us relentlessly works daily toward liberty, success will inevitably occur for us all.

SECTION TWO
THE WATER AROUND
THE BEND

Those Who Have Gone Before Us

Encouragement-Inspiration

WHO WILL SEE YOU AS THEIR LONE RANGER?

3 Lessons He Teaches That Are Still Important

We don't have to go back to those days of yesteryear to see *The Lone Ranger*. There are examples in our everyday lives if we observe and recognize them.

Growing up in a time of wholesome entertainment when parents didn't worry about what may show up on the television screen next was a blessing. It was easy to spot the good guys, and they always triumphed over evil. Unfortunately, our society became too "sophisticated" to appreciate the short and long-term benefits of those shows. Instead, producers demanded the unrestricted freedom to show anything and everything and push social agendas on the public.

One of the shows I enjoyed in reruns was *The Lone Ranger*. I'm sure part of it was because he was a Texan like myself, but I also appreciated him defeating the bad guys in every episode. Lost on the consciousness of my youth, but cemented into my sub-consciousness, were the other valuable lessons in each story.

I'll illustrate them with an experience of mine. In March of 2017, I was faced with a second heart procedure within four months. Since I detailed it thoroughly in **Unwelcome Opportunity,** I'll only highlight it here.

Because of potential complexities, I was transferred to a hospital in Round Rock, Texas. A doctor whom I had never communicated with arrived to solve my issue. We spoke briefly before the procedure and he candidly stated that he didn't know what he was going to find and he would figure out what procedure to perform in the operating room. Thankfully, I was at peace with my faith in God.

Later, I awoke and was briefed by another doctor about the successful operation. To this day, I have never again seen or spoken with the doctor who was my lone ranger. Why do I refer to him that way? Because I recognized, like my television hero, he showed up when I needed him most. He took care of my problem completely and then he left to help the next person without waiting for me to thank him.

Despite those who denigrate those old television shows as naïve, the moral messages they often delivered still work and are beneficial today. Whether you saw the show or not, each of us can be someone's lone ranger at any time.

Often, we are so busy with our daily demands that we miss the signals of opportunity. Other times, we may believe anything we might do won't make a difference.

Each of us has been given different gifts that together constitute a community positioned to help and support each other through the difficult times in life. President John F. Kennedy said, "One person can make a difference, and everyone should try."

Back in the 1960s and 1970s when the death penalty was suspended, north Texas juries were famous for handing out lengthy sentences to ensure the most heinous criminals wouldn't walk the streets again.

At one sentencing hearing, the judge handed down an 800-year prison term to a convicted killer. Before being led off to prison, the judge asked the man if he had anything to say.

Sheepishly, the felon stated, "Judge, I don't know if I can serve an 800-year sentence."

"That's all right," the judge responded, "just do the best that you can."

If we follow the judge's advice, we will make a difference in more lives than we might imagine, and the ripple effect will continue beyond our lifetime.

So today, and every day, let's look for and listen to those put in our paths whom we might help. Who knows, we might be the instrument used to answer their prayers.

In *the Lone Ranger*'s immortal words of yesteryear, **"Hi-Yo Silver, Away!"**

What are the 3 Lessons The Lone Ranger taught us that still apply?

- **Show up when someone is in trouble!**
- **Help those in need to overcome their problem.**
- **You don't have to be thanked to realize your impact.**

We shouldn't wait for a crisis to practice the attitude of *The Lone Ranger*. How many people will look at us and identify us as their lone ranger?

The Biggest Lie
in the World

Why are some lies bigger than others?

My father, Bill, imparted so much wisdom to me in bite-sized nuggets that at the time seemed like off-hand comments on events of the day. His style communicated the lesson in a way that I would receive it without putting up a child's defensive barrier to being taught something of importance.

For example, we would be watching someone on television and he would blurt out, "The biggest lie in the world is a half-truth." When I first heard the expression, I was too young to understand the depth of its meaning or what he was referring to at the moment.

As I grew older, he would explain the phrase when he used it. A politician might be speaking and citing numerous pieces of information. Mixed in with several truthful statements were one or more lies. The speaker was so smooth if you didn't listen critically and didn't check other sources, he could easily dupe you into believing the entire proclamation.

Smoothly spoken lies are not limited to politicians but occur in every corner of life. It can happen in personal or business arenas, and with people we have known a lifetime or have just met. Our only defense is a discerning and vigilant ear that tests what we hear against experience.

A corollary to an old expression would be that you can build 10,000 bridges but never be called an engineer. But, if you get caught in one lie, you will always be branded a liar.

Lies are not something that evolved during human history but go back to Adam and Eve in the book of Genesis in the Bible. God told them if they ate from the one forbidden tree that they would die. The serpent came along and misquoted God's command telling them they would not die but be like gods if they ate the fruit. The appeal of the forbidden fruit and the serpent's slick talk led them to a mistake that affected all of human history.

Not only will lies damage people for a long time, but they also inflict injury more rapidly than the truth supplies betterment.

As beloved as he was, Mark Twain had many detractors. Their negative statements led to his long-famous retort, "A lie can travel halfway around the world while the truth is putting on its shoes." His efforts to correct half-truths about him took a substantial amount of his time and effort. Imagine what more he might have accomplished if so many people had not injured him with falsehoods.

When I was a boy, Billie Sol Estes was infamous for his fraudulent business activities in west Texas. He was branded by people a liar, and he inflicted financial and emotional injuries to many people who had trusted him. He served multiple sentences in prison for his actions.

While I didn't know much about the details of his activities, every kid I knew was aware he was a liar. There was a younger boy in our neighborhood who told so many fibs during this time that all of the kids called him "Billie Sol" because no one could trust him. I wonder how long it took him to regain a positive reputation, or if he ever did.

Almost everyone can spot what some call a bald-faced lie because the presenter does nothing to mask it. Detecting and protecting ourselves from slick liars is much more challenging because they camouflage the lie with other truths. The other thing that makes uncovering a half-truth difficult is the ability of professional liars to tell their stories with a straight face.

President Ronald Reagan's adage about making sure the Soviet Union was truthful is just as valid today for anything presented to us as truth. He said, "Trust, but verify." What a simple but powerful tool to protect ourselves and others.

I hope you incorporate "trust but verify" into your standard procedure for receiving information.

BACK TO THE FUTURE
DEJA VU 2020!

Have you ever longed to go back in time to change current reality?

In the 1985 classic film, *Back to the Future,* Marty McFly was inadvertently sent back thirty years in a DeLorean time machine vehicle. The plot of the movie opened the viewer's imagination to the possibility of physically traveling back in time to improve the outcome of future events. It was ingenious.

The story entailed changing events related to Marty's parents and his future. He discovered his parents might not meet if he didn't intercede. His father was too nice to defend himself, and his mother was enamored elsewhere. Biff, who was his father's supervisor in the present, was a bully and threatened to prevent his parent's meeting.

A side story involved Goldie Wilson, a young café worker, whose ambition was to escape the café and achieve success. Marty subtly inspired him to consider becoming mayor of their town one day.

Potentially lost in the technology and excitement surrounding it was the most important point of the movie. After many challenges, Marty's parents finally connected.

Unknown until the end of the movie was the lesson for all of us. When Marty returned home, his brother and sister were successful and mature, unlike before his trip. His dad was a successful author, and his mother was happier and more positive also. Biff was reduced to detailing cars instead of bullying. Goldie Wilson did become mayor and was running for re-election in the present-day time of the film.

The reason for the changes? Marty influenced one thing each for his parents and Goldie during his trip, resulting in lasting changes in the future. The illustration is monumental but easily overlooked until one has enough journey behind them to look back and reflect on life.

I would like you to imagine traveling utilizing only your imagination not to a physical place, but to the place where ideals honoring all Americans and their values resulted in the most successful representative republic in the history of the world.

RICHARD V. BATTLE

We have never been a perfect country, but the first objective immediately after the words, "We the People" in the United States Constitution is, "in order to form a **more** perfect union." The founders acknowledged perfection was unattainable, but striving for "more" perfection of individual liberty and protection from tyranny was admirable.

Some would argue we have never been a great country, and the only way to become one is to discard our founding principles. I would proffer our original tenets were an excellent foundation, and our history includes mixed results of more and less freedom and government interference in our lives.

In the spirit of the *Back to the Future* film, wouldn't it be fun to see how things in the 21st century would differ with a few changes in the past?

- If we lost the Revolutionary War?
- If we lost the War of 1812?
- If President Lincoln would have allowed the South to leave the Union?
- If the Axis powers (Germany and Japan, after Italy surrendered) won World War II?
- If 9/11 had not happened?

As you can imagine, the list of possibilities is endless. While entertaining, energy spent considering any "what if" scenario is nothing more than that.

What interests me more is what I can do today to benefit others now and in the future. Each of us can create our own *Back to the Future* moments today that will change tomorrow. Even more fascinating to me is the fact that small, seemingly insignificant choices today can have gigantic results in our lifetimes and the lives of others. We have no way of knowing at the moment, but only in the reflection of the past can we see the affirmation of this truth.

In July 1944, no one could have imagined the impact of President Roosevelt's decision to replace Henry Wallace with Harry Truman as his vice-presidential candidate at the party convention. Less than a year later, Roosevelt was dead, and Truman was president. Truman made the fateful decision to utilize the atomic bomb on Japan, hastening the end of World War II. One of the reasons I appreciate his decision is because my father would have been very involved in a continuation of the pacific war.

Who knows what decision Franklin Roosevelt or Henry Wallace would have made about the bomb?

What can we do today that is the right thing to help others? Can you see the impact of other's past decisions? Can you see your decisions that have had more powerful impacts than imagined?

Oh, To Be Bulletproof Again!

Channeling Invincibility into Service

Do you remember the time in your life when you felt bulletproof? Did you use the feeling of invincibility to attempt some great achievement to advance man for the next one hundred years? Or, like I, and many others, did you risk life and limb over something you are now grateful to have survived and laugh about now?

A friend from college and I talked about individuals who were ignoring "social distancing" orders and living like there was no tomorrow despite the seriousness of the COVID-19 threat in the spring of 2020. Young people were validating the theory that every generation lives through a phase of believing they are "bulletproof" from any of life's risks.

A group from our alma mater, The University of Texas at Austin, illustrated the generational passage by traveling to Mexico via a chartered plane for spring break despite numerous government warnings against congregating in groups and travelling. Of the 100 plus students, 49 have contracted the virus as of this writing. Hopefully, their youth will enable them to survive the experience. Will they be able to laugh about the episode someday as my friend and I did when we recounted some of our adventures, or will they remember the horror of it?

My parents and grandparent's generation were less frivolous in activities that risked their bulletproof status because their lives were harder and more demanding than my boomer generation and those since. Living through the Spanish flu in 1918, the depression of the 1930s, World War II, and living off of their farm year-in and year-out forced my grandparents to mature quickly and live in a reality that was more demanding than I what have experienced. My parents missed the 1918 flu but endured the depression and World War II enough that it impacted their entire lives, and a lot of their thriftiness and prudence rubbed off on me.

Innumerable great achievements have occurred because adventurous individuals challenged the status quo at the risks of their lives. A few examples include Christopher Columbus, Lewis and Clark, Shackleton and the crew of Endurance, the Wright Brothers, Charles Lindbergh, the Doolittle Raiders, and astronauts in the space program.

Several flyers were lost in the pursuit of men flying and crossing the Atlantic. There is an adage among veteran pilots stating, "There are old pilots and bold pilots, but there are no old bold pilots." That is instructive. Those flyers dared over and over in the quest to improve the lives of their fellow man.

However, there is a fine line between adventurous, audacious, imprudent, risky, daring, foolhardy, reckless, and negligent behavior. Many pioneers, who just missed attaining the achievements listed above, and others, forfeited their lives in the grand effort.

My friend John suggested I write about some of our college exploits as we recounted them. Thankfully, we have attained the age where we "ought to know better" than to attempt those undertakings again (or new ones that are just a risky).

As some of you know, I have already written about hitchhiking from Lubbock, Texas, back to Austin. It occurred after a fight with a friend who attended a football game with John and me. My example of poor judgment included too much alcohol, hitchhiking a ride with a stranger, hopping a train, and a bus ride. I'm still grateful to have survived the trip as the train ride was 105 miles during the night while I was recovering from the alcohol and riding in the open-air between two chemical cars. It was an illustration of one of my too plentiful "knothead" experiences, which I admit to illustrate how I wish I had learned this lesson earlier in life.

Now, there is *Ripley's Believe it or Not*, and movies and such as *Jackass* celebrating daredevil activities that push the envelope of a devil-may-care attitude in unrewarding efforts to man even if they are successful. They desensitize us to the reality that life is brief and fragile.

Foolish risks like my story above illustrate the selfishness of the individual. Undue risks won't contribute to improving the lives of others are not worthwhile. If you're going to risk losing your life, do it in a grand enterprise that will advance civilization instead of salving individual pleasure.

The reality of the 2020 COVID-19 pandemic has restored an awareness of who the everyday real-life heroes are whose efforts provide us the necessities of life. They are not the movie and TV stars, athletes, singers, or others who have received adoration. They include the military, law enforcement, first responders, medical providers, farmers, food processors, truckers, distribution networks, grocery stores, pharmacies, oil and gas providers, power and water suppliers, telephone and internet companies, teachers, and restaurants.

While their day-to-day efforts have often gone unnoticed until this threat, many of them are risking their lives to minimize our deprivation and suffering. We owe them our utmost appreciation and gratitude.

It is up to us who have survived our ill-advised actions to temper the zeal of the next generations in a way that doesn't repel them from our advice. When we encourage people to channel their energy into endeavors larger than themselves, we can help lift the human spirit for years to come. If we can positively affect even a few people, we will have learned from our misadventures and contributed to progress.

RICHARD V. BATTLE

If that feeling of being invincible and bulletproof ever shows up in me again, I hope I'm smart enough to utilize it in service to the future of others instead of on my own desire.

There's a Goat in
My Dorm Room

Trust, but Verify

Isn't it funny how life is often stranger than fiction, and age-old sayings are always proven correct?

We're surrounded by stories daily in every form of media during our entire lives. Books, television shows and movies based on fantastic stories draw large audiences to them because of their entertainment value.

These stories can be based on large or small concepts or the past, present, or future. They will also invariably include natural and or supernatural beings. The anecdotes are dramatic, funny, or scary, depending on the subject and the target market. Isn't it amazing how fearful people can become from a story despite knowing it is mere fiction?

In 1938, Orson Welles broadcast a radio version of the H. G. Wells classic, *The War of the Worlds*, just before Halloween.

The performance sounded like a real news story, and it worked magnificently on thousands of people. People who tuned in after the introduction were terrified over the news that Martian spaceships had landed and were invading New York, New Jersey, and other locations.

A lot of listeners assumed it was a live news report and were scared out of their minds. People were stressed and shocked beyond anything they had ever experienced. Hospitals, police stations, churches, and newspapers were inundated with inquiries about what was happening, and what people should do to save themselves.

In less than an hour, it was over. The radio show so effectively incited fear in its listeners that outrage was a more common response than humor for those who were affected.

Maybe this is why Benjamin Franklin admonished us to, "Believe none of what you hear, and only half of what you see," many years ago. Especially now. The advent of special effects utilized in *Forrest Gump* enabled Forrest to appear alongside President Lyndon Johnson in a live picture. Maybe we shouldn't believe half of what we see any more without substantial proof.

RICHARD V. BATTLE

The illustration I want to share with you occurred when I was a freshman at The University of Texas at Austin. My roommate had grown up on a farm and regularly communicated how he missed the animals back home. I returned to the room on a spring Sunday afternoon after softball practice. When I opened the door, I questioned what I saw. There before me was my roommate and a live baby goat. I was astonished. I asked him to explain what the heck was going on.

He said he had been west of Austin at Hamilton Pool, which was then an unmarked and little-known oasis that we students frequented to get away from campus pressures. When he prepared to head back to our dorm room, he saw the baby goat and stated he had not seen any other goats in the area. He felt sorry for the baby and brought it back with him to care for it.

Startled and unprepared on how to respond, I didn't force the issue. By Tuesday, I was convicted and told him I would drive him and the goat back to the area on Friday after class. We would find a goat to take care of the baby. He reluctantly agreed to my plan.

Urgency increased the next day when housekeeping discovered the animal and communicated the infraction to the dean. My roommate received an order to get rid of the goat ASAP. Friday after class we made the drive back to the area where he found the goat. Instead of finding vacant land that stretched beyond our eyesight, we were welcomed with the vision of hundreds of goats as far as we could see. Angrily, I asked my roommate how he could have missed all of these goats and why he fabricated his story.

Sheepishly (pun intended), he confessed he couldn't resist the opportunity to have an animal of his own to take care of while going to school. We left the baby to find its mother or another substitute and returned to our dorm.

As you might expect, I didn't take him at his word after that episode, but always verified what he was telling me. Fortunately, we didn't get into any deeper trouble from the incident.

Years later, I attended the same church as Milton Reimers, who owned the land, including Hamilton Pool, before he made a deal for Travis county to acquire it. Since the goat in the story was his, I recounted the story, which he found most amusing after the fact.

People expect to take someone's word and to be able to trust them. I may appear cynical at times, but I remember the goat in my dorm room. I recall I should not blindly trust the stories presented to me without verification.

RICHARD V. BATTLE

GIVE ME A BREAK!

What great thing could you accomplish if you only received a break?

Like many words in the English language, the word break has multiple and sometimes opposite meanings. It isn't good if you break your leg or your car breaks down. However, receiving a break can be a good thing in other circumstances.

According to *The Free Dictionary by Farlex,* asking for a break can be a plea for someone to leave you alone, stop annoying you, or give you a concession or allowance. In other words, it can be used to ask for an advantage, consideration, or edge.

I can still remember attending a dinner while I was in college and hearing Lewis Timberlake present his speech "*How to Get the Breaks in Life"* for the first time. It mesmerized me. If you ever have the opportunity to listen to a recording of it, you will not regret it.

Little did I know I would eventually meet Lewis and he would become a mentor and life-long friend. Despite my exposure to many other, and often more famous speakers, Lewis Timberlake remained my favorite. The reason he was less well known wasn't because of a lack of excellence, but because he primarily spoke to corporations on a contract basis.

In his honor, I would like to share his principles with you, although there is no way to reproduce its electricity in written form.

If any of us want a break in life, we only need to remember the five letters of B-R-E-A-K.

First, we need to have a **BURNING DESIRE** to achieve whatever our dream or goal is and to pursue it relentlessly through adversity or storm. Too often, it is easy for all of us to discontinue our efforts, and sometimes we quit just before achieving the very thing we desire.

We can learn much from successful people and hasten our achievements. If we examine their lives more deeply, almost all have overcome failure and, in many cases, multiple times. Are you surprised to learn Walt Disney, Steven Spielberg, Mark Cuban, John Grisham, Albert Einstein, and Thomas Edison failed in efforts on their way to success?

Second, we need **REVERSICO!** Lewis said this was a Latin word that meant, "I flourish in adversity!" It is not an easy word to find, but Richard Harris utilized it in *The Journal* out of Georgia when honoring a late friend of his who used the same meaning.

When I first heard Reverisco used, I was around nineteen years old and only understood adversity in a theoretical sense. Like most of you, as I have aged, my understanding of the adverse challenges of life has grown more experientially, as I wrote about in **Unwelcome Opportunity** and **Surviving Grief by God's Grace**.

We will all experience trials and troubles in life. To succeed, we can't be defined by those challenges, but how we responded to them.

Third, we need **ENTHUSIASM**! As Ralph Waldo Emerson proclaimed, "Nothing great was ever achieved without enthusiasm!" If we are not enthusiastic about our pursuit of a dream or goal, it will be almost impossible to weather the trials, disappointments, and setbacks in its attempt.

Fourth, we need a **POSITIVE ATTITUDE!** While you may think this is closely related to enthusiasm it really isn't. You can be as enthusiastic as you want, but if you don't positively believe you can accomplish something, you will fall short of the effort. A positive attitude will also infect those around you and encourage people to support or join you in your effort. As Harvey Mackay said, "Positive thinking is more than just a tagline. It changes the way we behave. And I firmly believe when I am positive, it not only makes me better, but it also makes those around me better."

Finally, **KNOWLEDGE** enables us to successfully employ all of the characteristics to achieve our objectives. The world is changing at an increasing pace, which demands that we adapt to thrive going forward. The moment we discontinue our quest for knowledge and adapting to change, we sentence ourselves to a position that will diminish as rapidly as the amount of world knowledge increases.

I'm referring to more than book knowledge, although it is important also. We have the best opportunity to succeed when we understand human nature and complement our knowledge with experience.

All five of the characteristics forming the word **BREAK** have one thing in common. They all are dependent upon us to achieve them instead of our waiting for someone to give us something.

We are blessed to live in a country that provides us the liberty to live in the "pursuit of happiness" we define and desire, at the pace we decide to travel.

The next time you feel a break will help you achieve your dream remember what B-R-E-A-K signifies.

Thank you, my late friend and mentor, Lewis Timberlake, for your positive influence on my life!

THE SELF-DEFEATING
WORD THAT WILL DEMOLISH
YOUR DREAMS

What happened? Why did we misstep in our endeavor? Where should we look for the reason we failed?

When we fall short in any effort, we often look for the cause of the failure in a 360-degree circle around us. Sometimes we find targets of responsibility easily, and other times, it is a monumental effort identifying anything we can tag with the reason for missing our objective.

In reality, there are times the reason for our defeat is closer than we want to imagine. When we admit it, the limitations of our success are often self-inflicted and look back at us in the mirror. No one wants to concede to this truth, but our acceptance of it will lead to more successes than if we continue to mask our own contribution to the failure.

In my opinion, there is one word that has defeated the efforts of more people than the world's largest armies. It is another of those pesky four-letter words, but not a vulgar one, except in its affect on our path to success.

The word that I'm referring to is "can't."

When I was a boy, my dad gave me an ever-growing array of responsibilities as part of his teaching me to grow up into a responsible and mature man. Some of the lessons were more painful than others.

Upon reaching a point of failure I would exclaim, "I can't do that!" I didn't learn quickly enough that my statement would not result in being excused from the lesson. Rather than relief, I received additional instruction.

My dad, Bill Battle, would look at me and state with authority, **"Can't NEVER did anything!"** Instead of excusing me from pursuing the effort, he forced me back into it. Now my dad was even more committed to seeing me succeed in the achievement than previously, regardless of the time required, the pain I experienced, or the distastefulness of the process.

It must have been something about being part of the greatest generation as my parents were, because friends of mine received similar instruction from their parents.

How often do we limit ourselves before even attempting a dream by invoking the "I can't do that" excuse? Regardless of the number, it is too many. It is better to try and fail, than to never try at all. In fact, in nearly every circumstance, we will achieve more than we can imagine if we merely begin the effort and don't quit.

A far better example than my experience is Jennifer Bricker. She was born in 1987 without legs and put up for adoption. Her story of what a person can achieve with a positive attitude and perseverance should inspire us to attempt more rather than make us shrink thinking she is different than we are.

Jennifer's adoptive parents, Sharon and Gerald Bricker couldn't have realized their lessons for her would have a life-changing impact on untold thousands of people all over the world. They integrated her into their family, including three sons, and raised her as if she didn't have any limitations.

Their paramount instruction was to "**never say the word can't**." From an early age, Jennifer exhibited the results of the lesson that are so admirable and worthy of emulation. It was the greatest gift her parents could have given her.

She determined she wanted to become an acrobat and gymnast. Her father began working with her at aged seven on their trampoline. As you can imagine, she endured failure repeatedly at the beginning.

Undeterred, she persevered eventually winning state championships in high school for her power tumbling efforts. She also played softball and basketball and employed her skills in ways overcoming any perceived limitation.

When people asked her about her achievements despite her disability, she responded that she wasn't disabled.

Later, Jennifer discovered her birth family and her biological sister, was also the heroine who inspired her gymnastic endeavors, Dominique Moceanu. Truth is stranger than fiction, isn't it?

Now happily married, Jennifer is a professional acrobat, aerialist, speaker, and author of the inspirational book, *Everything is Possible*. She is a wonderful example of what we can achieve if we don't limit ourselves with the word "can't".

What dream do you desire? If you don't pursue it, will you regret it? If you pursue it and fail, will you achieve more than if you don't attempt it?

Who knows, you may achieve your dream and more, if you persevere until its achievement.

They Missed Me
by This Much!

Remember, how you felt, the last time you experienced a traumatic challenge or loss, and then survived and moved on from it? Looking back, were you better or worse off from what you experienced? Did the lessons you learned help you the next time you found yourself in trouble?

Those of you who remember the 1960s television show, or 2008 movie, *Get Smart* will recall the lead character's comment after escaping each life-threatening situation. "They missed me by this much," Maxwell Smart would recount, holding his thumb and index finger ever so close together. And, thus, he lived to fight another day. We chuckled at the line, but life has a way of showing up to all of us in ways that provide us the opportunity to recount that line after eluding perilous situations.

Many of you will remember the Indiana Jones movie series, which was a takeoff of many film serials before television where new chapters debuted every Saturday, and the hero would overcome one challenge only to end the episode in another life-threatening trap. Kids insisted on going back to the movie theater the next Saturday to see if and how the hero would overcome the entanglement and ultimately defeat the bad guys. Week after week, for two or three months, the story would unfold until the hero finally won the day.

Likewise, Indiana Jones journeyed from trial to travail throughout each movie. Of course, fans knew in their hearts that he would triumph. However, they all still experienced a modicum of suspense until the total victory was secured and the final credits appeared.

These stories are entertaining. The adventures of life however, are not assured victories like those of our screen heroes. Our tests show up as periodic episodes in our lives, if we are fortunate. I have written of many such experiences that I have encountered, and I will not belabor them here. Suffice it to say that I have been more blessed than challenged in this life, but I certainly have learned more from the adversities than I have the successes.

Some people live with their challenges every day. With no days off, their response to whatever uniquely defines their lives is an example on full display for others to receive instruction in navigating their temporary woes.

I recently learned of Tommy Morrissey, who has and is inspiring untold multitudes of people. He is far too young to realize the gift he is providing them. He is still writing his story. I have no doubt it will include a lifetime of encouragement for others.

Tommy was born without a right forearm. At a very early age, he preferred to watch golf videos with his dad instead of children's programs. By the time that he was three, he exhibited an unbelievable proficiency in swinging a golf club with one arm. Soon after that, he impressed the world's top golf pros with his positive attitude, determination and ability.

Tommy Morrissey is another example of the ability of humans to achieve more than they think they can. Encouraged by his parents, he focuses on what he <u>can</u> <u>do</u> instead of limiting himself with the debilitating view of what he cannot do. He exhibits the quote attributed to Jim Davis saying, "It's amazing what you can do when you don't know what you can't do!"

We can all live more fulfilling lives despite any disturbances we encounter along the way. Our choices when we experience those hazards will significantly influence our future steps and serve as an example to those observing us as a light to enrich their journey in life also.

How Can We Journey the Unknown Path after Challenges?

- **Practice the gift of gratitude after overcoming every adversity.**
- **Aim and proceed toward your next dream and goal, beginning with the end in mind.**
  - » **Don't live in past successes like the television shoe salesman Al Bundy.**
  - » **Don't be trapped by prior setbacks or failures.**
- **Act with optimism and a positive attitude.**
- **Persevere throughout all resistance until you accomplish your next objective.**
- **Focus on how your efforts will help others, and your successes, will multiple!**

Wouldn't it be great to live in a world where everything was 'nice' and we never experienced any difficulties? Well, as you know, that is only possible with the magic of Hollywood entertainment. We mortals have experienced troubles, and we will encounter more hardships along the way.

I hope the wind and sun are at your back when you next find yourself in rough waters. I am confident that your previous experiences will serve you to overcome each turbulence in the successful navigation of your journey.

Don't Fall for the Head Fake of False Hope!

Have you ever discovered the object you placed your faith, trust, and hope in was unworthy? Most of us would answer that question with a yes. Did you look for a new object the next time you searched for hope?

With rare exceptions, Chicago Cubs fans know the frustration of hoping their team will win a championship, only to be crushed year after year. Buffalo Bills fans experienced similar disappointment when their team reached four Super Bowl games only to lose each of them.

Head fakes are common in sports. There are few things more exciting in a baseball game than a well-executed hidden ball trick. Fake hand-offs, kicks, and punts happen in football often enough that a fake has to be extraordinarily special to elicit gasps in the crowd. These are all variations utilized in the old shell game that demonstrate the hand is quicker than the eye.

People also experience false hope in governments, media, businesses, organizations, science, education, and other institutions. Various sources tell us, "Don't worry, be happy," and "Trust us." Pardon me, but when I hear phrases like that, I buckle my chinstrap and expect them to abuse me. In nearly every instance, we always ask ourselves, "How could we have allowed them to fool us again?"

During my lifetime there has been a campaign to morph The United States government into the object people look to for safety, security, and the elimination of the risks of life.

One of the two camps responding to the 2020 COVID-19 pandemic utilized it in this manner, creating an illusion the national government will solve every problem, and no one will suffer any consequences from the vagaries of life.

The other camp responded to the threat to the country, aiming to minimize the loss of life, negative economic impact, and restoring economic and political freedoms, as quickly as possible.

RICHARD V. BATTLE

Media and other sources tell us the government will make life fair and secure world peace. As I wrote in *Conquering Life's Course*, "Life isn't fair!" It doesn't matter who leads, any level of government. They will not make life fair or assure us of world peace. Life has its ups and downs, risks and rewards, joy and suffering--and no one will change that.

My prejudice is this: I was educated in the time when most citizens still believed the fifth-biggest lie was, "I'm from the government, and I'm here to help you." Our distrust of government at all levels was handed down to us from our ancestors whose lives validated the experience our founders used in establishing our country.

After generations of increasing government overreach and "taxation without representation," 56 representatives declared independence from England based on a long list of grievances. After a seven-year war and period of a confederated government, another group wrote the constitution that has blessed us for so long.

Our founders weren't perfect, but they knew human nature. They instilled checks and balances, reducing the power any one person or small group could wield, which protected individual rights. As President James Madison said so well, "If men were angels, no government would be necessary."

Over time, and demonstrably so in my lifetime, individual rights have eroded for "the greater good" and by people's power grabs at all levels of government.

Don't get me wrong. I appreciate our representative republic, including the military, regulation of interstate commerce, and other constitutional functions. What I don't appreciate is a government that knows no limit to reach into my wallet and soul to deprive me of my economic and political freedom.

If we can't hope or rely on any human institutions, is there anything we can trust to live peaceful lives? Only an object of hope in something eternal and unchangeable is reliable in its power and trustworthiness. People of faith believe the object of their faith will deliver peace to them.

As a Christian, I believe the **Holy Bible** is immutable, and therefore trustworthy. Others believe in their faiths for a variety of reasons.

Before we commit to any article of faith, it is imperative we thoroughly test it for authenticity. Do you know why you believe what you believe? Can you confidently communicate your belief to others in a manner that doesn't pressure them to join you, but so they will understand you more completely? If you can't say yes to the preceding two questions, I encourage you to invest as much time and energy as it takes until you're able to do so.

~~~

How Can We Avoid Falling for the Head Fake and Discover True Hope?

- **Recognize no earthly institution is worthy of total trust.**
- **Understand that only an object that is unchangeable and eternal is trustworthy of our hope.**
- **Invest the time and energy necessary to confirm your beliefs.**
- **Know and be able to communicate why you believe what you do.**
- **Look for opportunities to share your ideas with others as you deepen relationships.**
- **Don't pressure others to agree with you, but to understand you better.**

Through the ups and downs of life, we make a vast number of decisions. No one is perfect, but hopefully, we learn through experience to reduce our number of regretful choices.

Regardless of the number of times that we fall for the head fake, or have missteps or failures along our journey, every day presents us new opportunities to strengthen our beliefs and the reasons we hold them steadfastly.

What You See May Not Be What You Get!

I know. You're thinking, *duh, this chapter is too obvious to waste my time reading.*

Like me, you may have been better prepared for some of life's surprises if you had been more vigilant.

I'm not perfect, or even close to perfect in practicing vigilance in my life. I'm amazed to reflect on lessons learned early in life that subconsciously prepared me for future experiences.

The first one I consciously remember was having my tonsils removed when I was three and one-half years old. I don't remember going to the hospital in Dallas, and vaguely remember the ice cream and presents afterward. But what I didn't see coming is chiseled vividly into my memory to this day.

One minute, I was in this strange place I later determined was the hospital. My mother and father were with me, and everyone was smiling. What could go wrong? In the next instance, two strangers deposited me onto a gurney. They proceeded to roll it down a strange hall away from my parents and to who knew where? As you might imagine, I let out a scream that probably woke people on the other side of the planet. I'm sure they tried, but I was inconsolable! I screamed non-stop, hoping in vain for my parents to rescue me.

The attendants wheeled me into a room with a bright overhead light. I squirmed and screamed as they next began to force a contraption over my mouth. I was sure it was to suffocate me. But I was no match for the medical team. I'm sure the doctor and nurses were relieved when the anesthesia took affect, and I lost consciousness.

Yes, I enjoyed the ice cream and toys I awoke to discover. But the experience also imbedded distrust in my mind toward adults. And it has served me well in most cases over the years.

As we travel to literal and figurative places beyond our sight, we need to prepare for as many potential surprises as possible.

My example serves as a humorous way to communicate a valuable life lesson. It's what you don't see that can hurt you. I was too young to understand or process what was happening to me. As adults, we must develop discernment. As *Merriam-Webster's* on-line dictionary defines, "**discernment** is the quality of being able to grasp and comprehend what is obscure."

Human nature is very trusting. It is common for us to accept what people tell us because we want to believe everyone is truthful. A sales rep whom I was coaching through a negotiation with an automobile dealer once informed me, "I have to believe what he told me." I instructed him, "Sometimes a person will only tell you part of the truth. They leave out other information that changes the entire meaning of the statement to obtain what they desire."

I believe discernment is a skill learned only after much practice and pain. After one learns good judgment, it is a valuable asset in life. Those without the skill of discernment often view those who have it as skeptics or cynics, and those who have it equally believe those who don't have it as naïve.

The opening scene from the iconic movie, *Jaws*, forever changed the perception of ocean swimming for those who saw it. An innocent young lady is enjoying an evening swim. Out of nowhere and without warning, an unseen shark attacks her. Her desperate attempt to repel the beast failed, and her life ended prematurely. As most of you know, the movie shark met his demise, but it didn't ease public tension.

I was scuba diving in Mexico after watching that movie, and I enjoyed it less than previously due to my anxiety about sharks. Instead of relaxing and enjoying the underwater paradise, I found myself stressfully looking for a great white shark. Thankfully, I have only seen one nurse shark during my diving adventures, but I continued to prepare ahead of my dives and remained observant while in the water.

Three years later, *Jaws 2* was released. It's marketing line, *"Just when you thought it was safe to go back into the water"* was brilliant. A new unseen terror appeared, and everyone's fears of sharks increased.

Unseen threats aren't always a shark or an operation, but can be as simple as a statement presented as a fact.

We face a daily hazard observing the news. Optimally, the story tells all sides. We interpret the story for ourselves. Classically trained journalists communicate the *who, what, where, when, why, and how* of a story.

These days, we see more and more opinions in stories. There is less and less *who, what, where, when, why, and how*. The selection of the story subjects covered and how much time they receive indicates the predisposition of the source toward them. It is easy for us to feel that what we're reading or hearing is all the newsworthy information. It is up to us to seek multiple sources and media platforms if we desire to achieve a well-rounded perspective.

Our challenge to see the unseen before it reveals itself to us is an on-going process of learning and preparation. Our individual skill development, benefits, us and our family, and all with whom we interact in our community.

How do we Acquire Discernment and its Benefits?

- **Recognize our natural tendency is to accept the messages provided to us at face value.**
- **Listen carefully to the information presented to you and how it is delivered.**
- **Consider the source of information and the agenda of the presenter.**
- **Seek confirmation of the information from independent sources.**
- **Use all of your senses and the information received to make your best decision.**
- **Learn from every decision to improve your skills.**
- **Share your knowledge with others for their benefit.**

SECTION THREE
TROUBLED WATER

Resilient and Relentless

WHERE DID THIS TURBULENT
WATER COME FROM!

Do you remember an adversity you encountered that seemed so large you would never overcome it? Have you overcome it yet?

If you have scaled your first challenge, did it infuse you with confidence for addressing future problems?

Not since the sudden attack on September 11, 2001 have we as a nation faced the same threat at the same time. The COVID-19 pandemic of 2020 arrived as suddenly as the terrorists who commandeered four airliners and turned them into flying bombs on that bright and blue-skied Tuesday morning.

Usually, we face troubles individually or in small groups. Those around us are often oblivious to our pain and suffering. We mask our misery to all but a select few. We enter, endure, and hopefully survive our hardships and live to fight another day.

When almost everyone is confronted with the same challenge simultaneously, there is no hiding it from anyone. People ask us how we are enduring it partially because they care for us, and the remainder ask in search for encouraging words for their own benefit.

The generation who have and are coming of age in 2020, for the most part, have never experienced adversity in the category their parents, grandparents, and great-grandparents overcame.

The COVID-19 global plague will be a life-defining moment for their generation like the 1918 Spanish flu, World War I, the great depression, World War II, the Cold War, the Cuban Missile Crisis, President Kennedy's assassination, and 9/11 was for their predecessors.

Their responses to the event are similar to older generations, but more intense because of their lack of previous experience. They are annoyed, frustrated, inconvenienced, uncertain, frightened, worried, and anxious almost universally. In the jargon of the day, they are "over it," meaning they want to escape it and don't want to deal with it at the moment.

Life-changing challenges appear in two different ways. First, a crisis appears unexpectedly, and suddenly out of nowhere and may be over in a short time. While the event may end quickly, it often spawns life-changing responses by those who experience it. The attack on Pearl Harbor in 1941 and the previously mentioned attacks on September 11th, 2001, are two well-known examples.

I was fortunate to meet Claudia Tangerife Castillo and communicate with her in Columbia virtually. Her book, ***The Tsunami of My Life***, is an inspirational telling of the December 2004 tsunami that claimed an estimated 280,000 lives in a matter of hours. It was an event of Biblical proportions.

Claudia's story put the reader into the scene as she lived this gut-wrenching experience. You are there before, and during the terrifying moments, the sea roared and wreaked havoc on so many. You struggle with her as she and her son escaped the aftermath and returned to their homes. Your emotions will rise and fall with her as if you were walking alongside of her step-by-step.

The event changed her entire life. Her story of endurance, escape, and rebirth as a life coach and author is a terrific example for all who want to break out of the pigeon hole they may be viewed in and pursue their dreams.

She tells us in *The Tsunami of My Life*, "The difference between where you were yesterday and where you will be tomorrow lies in what you think and do today." What great advice!

Her life mission is to share the lessons she learned with others through inspirational messages of resilience, perseverance, and overcoming adversity. She is using the troubled water she experienced to enrich the lives of all who hear her story and its message.

The second way life-changing events happen is through trials lasting for periods that seem like an eternity because we never know if or when they will end.

I related my experience of a three-year nightmare leading to my financial destruction in the chapter, *How Did You Spend Your Time in the Wilderness?"* Most people who never expected or prepared for financial setbacks experience additional stress when they occur. I learned and adapted from my loss. In the same way most people experiencing COVID-19 will be better prepared in the future as well.

There are many better examples of adaptability, resilience, and endurance that inspire me. At the outbreak of World War II, our parents and grandparents sacrificed their dreams to contribute to the survival of our country. Scores of actors and athletes like Jimmy Stewart and Ted Williams, joined their fellow citizens in volunteering to serve their country in the Army, Navy, Marines, Coast Guard or Merchant Marines.

When they left home, it was for the duration of the war. No one knew if we would win, how long it would take, or if they would return home. Communications with home and family were limited to letters, telegrams, and the rare phone call.

There were no breaks from the war zone and very few breaks within it.

After four years, it was finally over. Stewart and Williams sacrificed four years of their career and life but were more fortunate than others who made the ultimate sacrifice. Leslie Howard and Glenn Miller were two of the more noteworthy examples.

COVID-19 will pass. Years from now, it will reside in history like the Spanish Flu of 1918. When I was a child, no one discussed the Spanish Flu, and COVID-19 will be treated equally in the future. In the meantime, we have to face, endure, overcome, and learn from this challenge to build better lives in the future.

Lessons to Help Us Overcome Adversity From Those Who've Gone Before Us.

- **Deepen our faith and enhance our relationship with God.**
- **Dig deep into ourselves and attack the challenge head-on.**
- **Study successful people and adopt their methods of overcoming adversity.**
- **Come together with our family to aid each other.**
- **Unite in fellowship with our church to help and comfort each other.**
- **Prepare and save for a rainy day, or better yet, several rainy months.**

With so many examples of catastrophe in human history, why are younger people loathe to learn lessons to soften their suffering? As George Santayana and others so wisely said, **"Those who do not learn history are doomed to repeat it."**

We are wise to search the examples of those who overcame significant challenges and setbacks to recover more quickly and soar higher after our misfortunes.

This Isn't our First Rodeo

Why do we allow worry and fear to take a varying degree of control over our lives when a major economic collapse, disease, scares, or war occurs?

Being raised in Texas I often heard, "this isn't our first rodeo" from people to communicate their experience in the ups and downs of life and their confidence in successfully navigating whatever obstacle they were facing. It is one of the advantages of having more life experiences than others.

The 2020 Corona Virus pandemic isn't the first threat to our economy, security, and lives I have experienced; and like the others, we will survive and thrive again soon.

In my lifetime, the world was going to end:

- In October 1962, the **Cuban missile** crisis threatening nuclear annihilation occurred when I was in the sixth grade. We practiced hiding under our desks at school (as if it would have done any good). The memories below provided me the confidence to carry on my life.
  - » I focused on my parent's behavior to determine my level of worry. They remained calm, which enabled me to do likewise.
  - » We watched Walter Cronkite report daily throughout the 13 days to keep informed.
  - » My parents talked about the possibility of existing on a diet of Spam. They demonstrated their commitment to take care of me and my brother Jerry, regardless of what happened.
- In November **1963**, **President John F. Kennedy** was the first president in sixty years to be assassinated, which caused anxiety around the world with wonder how the United States would transition to a new president. It happened less than 20 miles from where I was at school. No reporters panicked despite televising Jack Ruby killing Lee Harvey Oswald on live television two days later.
- In **1974**, OPEC manipulated the oil market, and we were left to stand in line every other day to buy limited amounts of gasoline. It was somewhat painful, but we managed it and lived through it.
- The **1980's real estate collapse** ruined me financially.
  - » There was a three-year descent that obliterated my finances.

- » Those three years were extremely stressful, and it seemed as if they would never end.
- » Financial institutions received bailouts, and the big borrowers were able to refinance their loans, but there was no relief for small fish like me.
- On October 19, 1987, I checked in to my hotel in Memphis only to learn the stock market had dropped 22% in one day! While there was deep concern, there were no stories of people jumping out of buildings like 1929.
  - » My first appointment the next day told me he wouldn't buy from me because he wanted to wait to see how the market responded to the 19th. I laughed, and when he asked me why, I said no one had ever delayed buying because of the stock market in my experience.
- In **2000,** the **dot.com bust** caused those of us invested in the stock market to experience substantial losses.
- On the only **9/11** that doesn't require a year to identify it, terrorist attacks put our country into a hot war that no one knows if, when, or how it will end. It also caused a substantial financial market drop and significant volatility.
- In **September 2008**, the collapse of the financial markets and economic recession also hit many of our pocketbooks. Auto manufacturers, banks, and others received bailouts, but not the average guy on the street.

Throughout history, including in our country, events have erupted onto the scene that have caused anxiety and worry.

In addition to these events, I have personally experienced and survived an **apartment fire** where my neighbor died within thirty feet of me, **divorce**, **two heart procedures**, **cancer**, and the most significant loss of all, the **death of my only son**.

In the 1986 movie *Heartbreak Ridge*, Clint Eastwood starred as veteran U.S. Marine gunnery sergeant Tom Highway who was in charge of training a group of misfits into a toughened platoon who could handle any threat they were assigned. His techniques made them uncomfortable, which caused them to whine. Highway taught them that no matter what happened; they must Adapt, Improvise, and Overcome to succeed. We must do the same to survive our challenges in life.

What can we do to keep our children and ourselves calm and resilient?

- **Be Informed**
  - » Big events are fluid.
  - » Watch levelheaded reports, not sensationalized versions.
- **Be Prudent**
  - » Differentiate essential vs. optional activities.
  - » You can delay some things and not others.
- **Be Prepared**
  - » Don't buy a truckload of toilet paper, but do have a few days of supplies of whatever you need.
- **DON'T PANIC!**
  - » Your children will look to you and mirror your attitude about the threat.

- **Don't worry about what you can't control!**
  - » If you can't control it, prepare to adapt to the outcome.
  - » Things are rarely as bad as we fear.
  - » Many things we fear never occur.
  - » As the late Lucille Braden said, "Worry is interest paid on a debt before it is due."
- **Think back to what you worried about three years ago. Do you remember?**
  - » "This too shall come to pass," as told about so many other events in Scripture.

When you are in the middle of the storm, seeing beyond it is tough. Know that no challenge is infinite in size or time.

We will survive and thrive again soon!

What can we do today to prepare for the next unplanned, untimely threat to our family? What can we do today to survive and thrive in an unwelcome future event?

WHEN TOUGH TIMES ARRIVE: WHY "WHY" ISN'T THE RIGHT QUESTION

What is the last tough time you experienced? Was it your first trial, or have you walked through the fire before? Did the latest challenge freak you out, or were you able to endure and survive it with confidence?

Looking back, the shocking helicopter crash on January 26th, 2020 that took Kobe Bryant, his daughter, and seven other lives might have served as a foreshadowing for the global alarm caused by the arrival of COVID-19 (Corona Virus) in early 2020.

The accident received more publicity because of Kobe Bryant's celebrity status, but it brings the reality into everyone's consciousness that anyone can pass from this world at any time.

All nine of the victims of the helicopter crash left behind people who loved them, and each had very long lives ahead of them. Their sudden departure makes people realize their mortality in addition to their grief for those lost.

While people mourned the loss of Kobe Bryant and the others, for most it was not a personal loss. With COVID-19, everyone will experience a loss of control in their lives, suffer economically, and many will know or personally experience the loss of good health or their lives.

The common question asked when someone suffers or someone they know dies prematurely is, "Why"? After I lost my only son in 1998, I faced a reality I had never contemplated. After a long search for comfort that my son was in heaven, my faith assured me God was in control, and I discovered there were more important questions to ask. **I realized I did not grieve where my son was, but where he wasn't.** I was then able to process my grief and resume living.

Part of my grief journey resulted in writing the 2002 book *Surviving Grief by God's Grace* with the mission to share my experience with others to help them with their suffering and grief.

I learned in Proverbs, "Trust in the Lord and lean not on your own understanding," and in Deuteronomy, "The secret things belong to the Lord our God". Those lessons made me realize "why" wasn't as important a question to ask as **"What Now"?** The "why" question looks solely in the rearview mirror, where there is only a past to trap you.

In other words, I don't know why something happened, and I can't change it, but I am here for a reason to deal with it.

The **"What Now"** question looks forward to a future where our daily decisions will significantly impact our lives and the lives of all of those we touch directly or indirectly.

We should learn lessons from our good and bad life experiences. If that is true, what lessons are each of us to learn from our COVID-19 experience?

While each of us may learn individual lessons that prepare us to face future life-threatening events, one I shared in *Surviving Grief by God's Grace* is one we should all recommit to every day: "Life is a gift. Value every moment." Dr. Haddon Robinson said it this way, "Time is our enemy disguised as our friend." Tell your loved ones you love them. Invest time with them because "relationships are the most important thing in life."

As we live day-by-day during this life-altering episode of a world-wide pandemic, it is my prayer you will receive comfort and peace from the Spirit, and be examples to others in how to deal with uncertainty, lack of control and the unbridled emotions of others. I hope you will discover lessons from this event that will bless you and those you touch in the future.

It is inevitable we all will experience an **Unwelcome Opportunity** or many of them during our lifetime. How we respond to them is what matters. How will you face your next challenge? Will it be easier to weather the storm because of your unwanted experience?

Surviving and Thriving the Black Hole of Anxiety and Grief

When was the last time you experienced the peace of controlling your life? How have you felt when you found yourself in the black hole of the unknown? How did you respond when you looked into the face of anxiety and grief?

Usually, we face challenges and trials alone or in small groups. When we interact with others, we may be unaware of the pain and suffering they are experiencing. Our lack of awareness prevents us from helping them, and we may add to their discomfort by making an otherwise harmless comment or action.

The 2020 COVID-19 pandemic has thrust everyone globally into a common, unsettling place. Very few alive have previously faced such a universal health threat. Although we all face the same menace, there will be a variety of responses and results we each experience.

Anxiety

People are undergoing varying levels of **anxiety,** depending on the life events they have previously endured. For so many, there is no previous experience of trials, much less, multiple threats to their comfortable lives.

There are three contributors to anxiety that individually are disturbing enough, and in maximum combination can be debilitating.

Governments dictate some activities and limit others. These acts influence people, making them feel like they have lost control of their lives. It is as if the footing under us is uncertain, and the next step may increase our suffering.

If we aren't in control of our lives, is anyone? Our level of faith in a controlling force beyond ourselves will substantially differentiate our ability to process the realization we aren't in control of what is occurring.

Compounding our **loss of control** is the **uncertainty** of what will happen next. When will our perception of control return?

When will things return to normal? Will those making the big, life-changing decisions make ones that will help or hurt the situation?

How will I respond to the **unknown, inevitable changes** that will come? Can I adapt sufficiently or quickly enough? Will I prosper or suffer?

Grief

Besides, the increased levels of anxiety, many people are **grieving** more than usual during this international crisis. Family dysfunction, divorce, loss of health, suicides, and death are occurring at increased rates and to people who haven't previously encountered them. The 2020 pandemic has also increased people's feelings that they or a loved one may quickly and unexpectedly pass from this life at any time.

While I appreciate the education I learned through divorce, two heart procedures, cancer, and the loss of my only son, I wish I had not lived those episodes in my life.

The first response from most of us when we suffer is, "Why me?" This question looks back into our past for an offense justifying our punishment. Too often, people entrap themselves with a past guilt that cripples their futures. No cure or growth comes from living in past actions.

I believe the correct question to ask when suffering arrives is "What now?" In other words, what am I supposed to learn to improve my future and help others who find themselves in similar positions? There are three major benefits of this approach. First, it focuses on the future, which is all we can influence. Second, it spotlights what we can do to improve ourselves. Finally, by focusing on assisting others, we will pity ourselves less and be servant leaders.

The second major lesson I learned that helps me grieve those I have lost is **I don't grieve where they are, but I do grieve where they aren't.** My faith provides me the peace to trust my loved ones are safely in heaven, and I will reunite with them one day. My grief is really about being separated from them presently on earth. In the long-term perspective, it is a short time.

Our Response

Our choice is how to deal with anxiety and loss. That decision will significantly impact how we emerge from the void into the next phase of life in this world.

We can hunker down and pass the time with substances or entertainment, wishing the uncertainty will leave, and the prior order of life will return unchanged. I believe those choosing that path will awaken in the new reality. They will wonder what happened and how others leapfrogged them by making different choices.

The other choice we have, through necessity or imagination, is that we will discover new gifts unveiled to adapt to the world delivered to us. We will plan, prepare, implement, adjust, and thrive regardless of the amount of change encountered, or loss we endure. Our forefathers, who suffered mightily through pandemic, depression, and world wars, have shown us the way, and we stand on their shoulders.

I plan to be in the second group, which will better my life and hopefully broaden my shoulders for future generations to benefit also.

How Can We Best Emerge and Thrive from the Void of a Black Hole?

- **Expect to experience loss of control, uncertainty, and change in life.**
- **Anticipate those events and prepare yourself.**
- **Don't panic when life throws you a curveball.**
- **Adapt your activities to survive until you're able to regain control.**
- **Respond to future shocks in life with more confidence from your experiences.**

Hopefully, like other life scarring events, we'll be able to look back and see not only the hardships, but the benefits we have gained from the COVID-19 predicament. There is no rainbow without the rain, and we don't develop endurance without the sacrifice of building strength through exercise that pushes us beyond our comfort level.

We Need Hope
More than Ever –
Where Do We Find It?

Who would have thought in early February 2020, the world would turn upside down with a pandemic that threatens to decimate untold numbers of lives and upend the way of life of virtually everybody?

While some alive today have lived through world wars, depression, famine, and pestilence, the COVID-19 virus is threatening us in a different way than those experiences.

Fear, uncertainty, doubt, apprehension, anxiety, and any other number of words expressing people's lack of control over their lives seem insufficient to describe the emotions being felt by so many at this time.

People less experienced in the trials of life are learning lessons that include:

- **Control is an illusion.**
- **Hope in self for peace is futile.**
- **No government is powerful enough to rely on for peace and safety.**
- **There is nothing on this earth that will provide rest and peace in the darkest hour.**

Who am I to write about these dour prognostications and stimulate the question, "Where can I invest my hope for today and eternity?" My many successful experiences in my life bless me, but the trials and tribulations I have endured better prepare me for today and tomorrow. They enable me to share the painfully-learned lessons with others, hoping to make their paths smoother.

My experiences include surviving an **apartment fire** where my neighbor died less than 30 feet from me, and experiencing **financial ruin** with the Texas real estate collapse in the 1980s, **divorce**, **two heart procedures**, **surviving cancer** and enduring my most significant loss of all, the **death of my only son**.

I know for myself and believe the only Hope that is satisfying in any circumstance is available and close at hand. I place my hope in the God of *The Holy Bible* confidently because of the many times He has loved me more than I deserve, provided me all I have needed, and carried me when I could not walk.

My reliable personal experience and evidence of my savior Jesus Christ, the Holy Spirit, the Scriptures, and examples of fellow believers cement my faith for provision to withstand any trial.

When the last institution has let you down and you feel your most hopeless, my desire for you is that you will find the only Hope that will be there for you wherever you are, with whatever you need and whenever you need it.

Below are six Scriptures that lifted my spirit through my most difficult days. May you find comfort, peace, and hope in them also.

Isaiah 40:31 - but those who **hope** in the LORD will renew their strength. They will soar on wings like eagles; they will run and not grow weary; they will walk and not be faint.

Jeremiah 29:11 - For I know the plans I have for you," declares the Lord, "plans to prosper you and not to harm you, plans to give you **hope** and a future.

Romans 12:12 - Be joyful in **hope**, patient in affliction, faithful in prayer.

Romans 15:4 - For everything that was written in the past was written to teach us, so that through the endurance taught in the Scriptures and the encouragement they provide we might have **hope**.

Romans 15:13 - May the God of **hope** fill you with all joy and peace as you trust **in him**, so that you may overflow with **hope** by the power of the Holy Spirit.

Hebrews 11:1 - Now faith is confidence in what we **hope** for and assurance about what we do not see.

I sincerely believe we will weather this storm, and life will return close to its former shape for most of us. If it does, how long will it be before the lessons we learn through this event are forgotten?

When the next tribulation arrives, will our past experiences and the education we received from COVID-19 have us prepared? Can't we prepare mentally, emotionally, and spiritually for future trials with the same zest as we might stock food, secure shelter, and formulate our security plan? Can't we share the experience with our children for them to remember, like our parents presented us the 1930s depression, the world wars, the holocaust, Hiroshima, 9/11, and other earth-shaking events?

Each of us has a choice in how to respond to the tribulations of life. Mine is to maintain a positive attitude, learn the lessons from each trial, and to encourage others in the hope they will survive their challenges and flourish.

"What you do in the present, will create a past that will greatly influence your opportunities and dreams in the future." – from *The Four-Letter Word that Builds Character* by Richard V. Battle, 2006.

How Did You Spend Your Time in the Wilderness?

5 Beneficial Lessons for Times of Uncertainty

How long did it take you to want out of the wilderness? Was it a profitable experience or time wasted?

It isn't too uncommon for individuals to find themselves in the wilderness during their lifetime, but it is extraordinary for almost the entire planet to find ourselves here in the Spring of 2020 with the Corona Virus (COVID-19) pandemic.

I have endured enough life experiences that I should have credentials as a social scientist. Observing the unique common reality of the Corona Virus pandemic and how people experienced it is fascinating for me.

Two examples I dread recalling (but are instructive and were tied together), happened during the 1980's real estate crash in Texas. I had invested in rental real estate for over seven years and was on my way to building a substantial portfolio. The 1986 tax reform bill significantly changed the economics of investment real estate within ninety days of its enactment. Month-after-month for three years, I watched my savings dwindle while I tried to save my properties. Every month, I prayed for things to turn around, and for the stress and financial loss would end. A friend of mine and I joked that we had experienced all of the character building we could stand, and if we could get out of the trap, we wouldn't make the same mistake again.

In the middle of this time period, the Internal Revenue Service (IRS) began an audit that eventually covered two years because my expenses had also increased significantly to maintain the properties. In a tax audit, there is no time limit, and the sense it would never end was inescapable and oppressive. Thankfully, after twenty months, they concluded their investigation. I owed them a mere $ 200.00 for a math error. The non-financial costs to me were incalculable.

That period was painful financially, physically, emotionally, spiritually, and on any other level, I have thankfully forgotten since then.

Now, in the spring of the 2020 Corona Virus pandemic, nearly all of us find ourselves out of control, emotionally stressed, financially burdened, uncertain of the future, and interacting with other people who are facing the same demands with a variety of experiences and perspectives to deal with it.

We all will choose how we respond to this unique time in our lives. Will we allow our stress to paralyze us, so we waste this time? Or, will we make the best of the situation and turn it into an opportunity to grow and prepare for the post-pandemic world?

The people who proactively use the available time and resources to grow and develop will emerge and flourish because of their preparation. Those who waste their time, thinking and worrying about things they can't control, will squander their time. They will emerge wondering what happened and how others reaped the rewards they missed.

Last week, I watched the annual holy season broadcast of *The Ten Commandments*. In addition to enjoying the story and spectacle, each time I view it I discover something new that helps me. Watching the movie this year, it struck me when Moses fled Egypt after killing an Egyptian and spending forty years in the wilderness before God called him to lead his people out of bondage. How did Moses deal with his exile?

While it wasn't purposeful to leading the Jews, Moses spent his time in Midian learning about God and his people, reflecting on his life and purpose, listening for God to speak with him, and then obeying God when his surprise call came to return to Egypt.

Although he didn't feel worthy of leading his people out of Egypt to freedom, he was the chosen instrument to do so.

Then, he led his people for another forty years in the wilderness as they wandered around after their disobedience and lack of faith. Imagine being one of those Israelites who were uncertain of how long they would wander in the desert, where they would go, or end up? And we think a short period of uncertainty is cataclysmic!

What 5 Lessons benefit us in times of uncertainty?

- Focus on what you can control and find activities preparing you for the future.
- Avoid idle time. It is the devil's workshop. Proven repeatedly.
- Maintain a structure for your days and the discipline to persevere each day.
- Remember things can always be worse. We don't have to look far to see others worse off than we are.
- Think, about how you can help others. The more we think about others, the less we focus on any negatives in our lives.

Whether we emerge from this or a future wilderness soon, or if it takes a long time, what can we do each day to survive, thrive, and encourage our family and friends?

How Did I Get Into
This Mess?

Did you ever stop what you're doing and ask yourself, "How did I get into this mess?"

Sometimes we get ourselves into a mess with a poor decision, but there are other times we find ourselves in a mess because we were not aware of what was going on around us.

I joke with people that I can't get into the messes I want to get into, and can't get out of the ones I wish I could have avoided.

The 2020 Iowa Democratic caucus is one example where planning wasn't followed-up, and the Democrat Party and Iowa were embarrassed because of their incompetence creating an app for people to vote through their personal devices. Weeks after the caucus date, the simple task of counting the votes of 170,000 people remained unfulfilled.

I believe the primary caucus had been conducted so many times without a hitch, that leaders felt they didn't see the need to pay attention to the details even though they were implementing a new technology. Or, I could be wrong, and they were just plain incompetent.

I don't mean to only pick on Iowa or anyone else because I have found myself in more messes because of my poor decisions or from missing the obvious than I would like to admit to anyone.

One that is humorous now, but frightened me exceedingly at the time, happened on a company trip to Morocco in early 1979 before the Shah of Iran fell and Muslim tensions with America escalated. It was also before you could prepare yourself thoroughly on the internet for all of the "fun" the locals had waiting for tourists when they arrived.

One of our activities included a visit to the Jemma el-Fnaa (market square) in Marrakesh. I found myself exploring it alone as I was traveling solo with the group. I wandered through the covered alleyways bordering the square without incident. Then, I decided to visit the open-air central market and take in the local culture.

At that time, if you took the picture of a resident in Morocco, you were expected to pay the person for the privilege. I had done so in other locations, and I anticipated doing so again.

Toward the center of the square, I saw a group of snake charmers who were playing their wind instruments. Just like in the movies, the snakes lifted themselves out of their baskets, or off of their mats. They were captivated by the music. I found one I liked, snapped a picture, gave the piper some money, and turned to leave.

Almost immediately, I heard a voice call out from behind me, and then I made my mistake. As I turned to see if it was me who the man called, the man looped a cobra over my head, and the bearer held its head and tail against my belly button. I was stunned and shocked. The man put his other hand out, asking for money. My initial response was to point to the seated charmer I had just paid and say I had already provided payment for the picture.

He would not relent. An angry look came upon his face. Having no wingman to assist me led me to dig my right hand into my pocket as far as it would go and extract all of the money in that pocket. When I presented the money to him, he released the snake's tail from his grasp, turned, and walked away with his snake, looking for his next prey.

I scanned the horizon looking for sanctuary. Fortunately, there was a rooftop café close by, and I retreated to it quickly to wait for my friends so we could board our bus and get out of Dodge.

Driving back toward Casablanca, I spied an American flag off of the road. It stood at a United States Marines outpost. It was a welcome sight, and I thought long about enlisting that day.

Upon my return home, I had my pictures developed, and I examined the photograph of the snake that caused me so much anxiety. The photo showed the snake and the seated man I had photographed, and beyond, dressed in white, was the man who wrapped the second snake around my neck. You can see him below in the center of the picture.

Oh, had I been more observant! Oh, had I not been alone in the market!

I have mixed memories of Morocco, but I would never go back there again!

One of my favorite examples of a mess occurred in the terrific movie, **No Country for Old Men.** In it, the deputy takes the sheriff (Tommy Lee Jones) on a horseback examination of the scene where a drug deal went bad. Scattered across the countryside were dead humans and dogs, vehicles that had received numerous gunshots, and spent shell casings all around. As it had happened a few days before, nature was proceeding to decompose the bodies, and flies were everywhere.

In a tough scene to watch, the deputy finally stated to the sheriff, "Well it's a mess ain't it, sheriff?" Tommy Lee Jones, with a straight face and straighter delivery, replied, "If it ain't, it'll do till the mess gets here."

How many messes do you remember being in because of a poor decision or not paying attention to your surroundings?

What can we all do to avoid finding ourselves in the situation where we ask, "How did I get into this mess?

I Just Got Fired!
Now What?

What would you do tomorrow if you lost the career position that you love today?

Thankfully, I never experienced this traumatic loss, but observing and learning from others prepared me for its possibility. I witnessed events that prepared me for my post-corporate career which has provided me fulfillment and freedom beyond my imagination.

The lesson came in three phases from three close friends who provided me with totally different experiences from which to learn from them.

The late 1990s was buzzing with technology developments, which fueled an explosion of start-up companies. They operated with an urgency to succeed or get bought by a larger organization before they failed.

C.B. Huchingson and I had worked together in two previous organizations. He called one day to inform me that he had left his vice president position in another organization. What he said next caught me off guard. "When are you going to find me a new job," he inquired? Being younger than he and at a position lower than the one he had been in made me wonder. How was I going to find a job for him?

He was the first one to enlighten me that with rare exceptions, **once you were in your forties or older, the only way you would find a corporate job was through a friend**. It was a lesson that would be reaffirmed repeatedly over the years.

Fortunately, I was the friend that helped find him his next job, and ironically, it was the one I eventually earned and held until the end of my corporate career. You never know how helping a friend will someday help you.

In 2000, the dot-com crash occurred, and thousands of people found themselves out of work in a shrinking market. What I observed from many examples provided me my second great lesson in case I lost my job.

I discovered my friends and others, like myself, were so focused on excelling at their careers and planned to work at their current organizations until their retirement. Very little contingency planning was explored to answer the question, *what if I lose my job today?* That lack of preparation would be costly in more ways than I can include in this story.

When the fatal day came, people who had invested everything into their work went into a deep state of shock. They did not deserve to lose their job, and that was common for most who experienced job loss during this time. Almost all of them went through up to six months of grief before they began searching for their next opportunity.

My lesson was to plan for the question, "***What I would do if I lost my job today?***" I developed a plan I could implement from day one if necessary, and reaped peace of mind by doing so. That plan became my post-corporate career.

The financial meltdown of 2008 provided additional education opportunities. It forced me to release two of my managers with whom I had worked for twenty years, and who were dear friends. It was the worst task I had to perform in my entire business career.

Bill Gardner was a little older than I and began bombarding online job sites with his resume. I shared the lesson I had learned from C.B. Huchingson's experience and suggested he contact his vast network for opportunities. He only did that after he exhausted the internet search, but it bore fruit almost immediately. Bill's experience reinforced the lesson about finding jobs through your friends after surpassing the age of forty.

Joe DeRossi walked a different path and found another job and continued his success. Later, I was able to rehire him in a sales position, which was below the level he had previously occupied. My concern was whether his ego would allow him to perform well.

Not only did Joe put aside his ego, he rapidly became a top performer year-in-and-year-out. Joe is a terrific example of handling rejection from an organization and returning to it and becoming a significant contributor to its success. I never saw anyone respond to adversity as well as Joe did. He showed **what is possible if you can put your ego aside, focus on the opportunity at hand, and apply yourself to it.**

I hope you never unexpectedly lose a career job. If you do, I hope the example of my friends will help you prepare to face, and thrive, from your experience.

Victim or Overcomer – It's Our Choice!

Despite the myriad of outside influences on daily life, it is the choices we make that predominately impact our futures.

We choose whether to declare ourselves a victim of life or an overcomer of whatever life deals us.

Let's examine and compare three differing viewpoints between victims and overcomers.

Victims dwell in fear, which paralyzes their ability to progress. Their focus on the negative outcome of every situation results in decisions minimizing risk and action. Failure results in reinforcing their fear and reproducing itself in future decisions. Without a drastic change, it is an endless loop of self-fulfillment.

Confident people realize success won't result from every decision, but it will occur more often than failure and is worth the price because it enhances the exploration of life.

The 2016 movie, *Hacksaw Ridge* re-introduced Desmond Doss, his principles and heroism to a new generation. When the United States entered World War II, Desmond felt a duty to country and volunteered for the Army. His religious beliefs forbid his even holding a rifle, which created many conflicts with his fellow soldiers and Army leadership. He could have taken the easy way out and returned to civilian life.

However, his devotion to service was so great that he became a medic and deployed to Okinawa, Japan with the soldiers who harbored immense disdain for him. Fighting to claim the Maeda Escarpment (real name for Hacksaw Ridge) was brutal and the territory changed hands between the American and Japanese multiple times.

One time, Doss remained on top of the cliff overnight, rescuing wounded soldiers and lowering them to the base of the cliff for medical attention. He kept praying, "Lord, let me save just one more," repeatedly, and even saved a few enemy soldiers. Eventually, seventy-five men were saved!

On a return assault to the escarpment, Doss was wounded by a rifle and received seventeen pieces of shrapnel from a grenade, which ended his service in combat.

He was the only conscientious objector to earn The Congressional Medal of Honor for his service. As you can imagine, soldiers who served with him became devoted friends because of his choice of self-sacrifice as he lived his life with confidence because of his faith.

Victims tend to rationalize their position in life, which leads to stagnation. Eventually, they metaphorically drown to any growth and enjoyment.

Relentless is how I describe confident people who pursue their dreams and life despite obstacles. We are not promised an easy life, and very few people are fortunate to avoid the challenges of life. In the immortal words of Billy Clyde Puckett, the hero of *Semi-Tough*, "Nobody said it wasn't going to be semi-tough." This phrase served as inspiration for himself and others to persevere through turbulent times.

When we expect periodic setbacks, we will refuse to succumb to them but will turn their lessons into future successes.

Finally, victims never overlook an opportunity to excuse their place in life or anything that happens to them. Their negative self-focus paralyzes them and demotivates those they encounter. My best advice on dealing with negative people is to have as little contact with them as possible so your efforts won't be adversely affected.

If you befriend positive people who accept responsibility and survive challenges, your resulting positive attitude will stimulate your efforts to higher levels. Studying commonalities of successful people will confirm the benefits of living with a positive attitude regardless of your situation.

Travis Mills was a twenty-five-year-old soldier on his third deployment to Afghanistan when a bomb exploded, resulting in him being a quadruple amputee. His initial depression about his future led him to tell his young bride, Kelsey, it was okay for her to move on with her life.

She refused his offer and rededicated herself to their marriage! Her story of love and devotion to him is as heroic as his!

Returning to the same perspective that made him a successful soldier, he pushed his recovery and rehabilitation beyond medical timetables. He fed himself after five weeks and took his first steps after seven weeks with prosthetics.

He now spreads the message of his good fortune to audiences as a motivational speaker. His admonitions are:

1. Don't dwell on the past.
2. You can't control every situation, but you can control your attitude.

He admits others have suffered more than he has, which is true for nearly all of us. He exemplifies overcoming a significant setback, and his attitude is worthy of our emulation.

How do we become an overcomer instead of a victim?

- **Live confidently acknowledging misfortune will occur.**
- **Learn from every challenge or failure to succeed next time.**
- **Expect life to be "semi-tough" some of the time.**
- **Take responsibility for your choices.**
- **Relentlessly live and pursue your dreams regardless of defeats.**
- **Be an example to others to imbue them with confidence for their life journey.**

Every day we make multiple choices that potentially affect the rest of our life and all of those people we influence. What can we do today to make each one better?

Nuts!

When you're in a pickle and looking for advice on how you should respond to the pressure, what should you do? Whose voice should you listen to for help?

We all find ourselves in situations where we look for the help of others to reinforce a decision we have made, or to influence us in a decision ahead of us. Who we listen to in those critical junctions of our lives will have a disproportionate effect on our future.

Well-intentioned friends can promote caution for us to avoid the pain of failure. The bigger the risk of our moment, the louder their voice urges caution. Our well-wishers rarely look at the opportunity of the reward because they have little faith that we can realize it.

Discouragement kills more enthusiasm, squanders incredible amounts of energy, and thwarts the advancement of civilization by killing or delaying the development of many ideas.

Attempting a grand objective usually results in a superior achievement, even if the goal is missed, compared to no effort at all. As the Native American proverb states, "It is better to aim at the sky and strike an eagle than to aim at the eagle and strike a rock."

Other friends push us forward, seeing only the potential of a great reward and avoiding any consideration of the risks and costs of failure. They also wish us well, but we must possess discernment to temper their enthusiasm.

Some of my greatest achievements occurred because friends pressured me to attempt something that I had not thought of on my own. In 1981, my late, long-time friend, Richard Wroten, told me that if I didn't become the president of the Austin Jaycees in the future, he would kick my rear end. I had never envisioned that possibility for myself.

After Richard's encouragement, I modified my path and achieved the office. A team of several hundred volunteers, who became life-long friends, accomplished a monumental record that year. I was privileged to lead the team and realized a life-changing experience. If I had ignored my friend's forceful encouragement, I would have missed the opportunity. I have benefitted from experiencing other examples where friends have boosted me to achievements that I never thought possible.

On the other hand, I have also had experiences where I followed advice leading to failure. My most painful experience occurred in the Texas real estate market in the 1980s. I had been encouraged to invest in rental real estate. Friends in the business who meant well inspired me to add to my portfolio, believing the market could only go up. Their advice was good until the United States Congress modified the tax law in 1986, the market crashed, and the downward spiral of my modest real estate empire began.

Brigadier General Anthony McAuliffe, the Deputy Commander of 101st Airborne Division in World War II, found himself in the tightest of spots. His unit was surrounded by the German army during the Battle of the Bulge in December of 1944. The Commanding officer, Major General Maxwell Taylor, was attending a staff conference in the United States when the German offensive began, which left General McAuliffe in command.

After days of attacks by the Germans, weather so bad air support was unavailable, and no sign of reinforcement, McAuliffe's dilemma arrived. The American Army was hanging on to Bastogne by their fingernails. German officers approached American lines under a flag of truce. They presented General McAuliffe a surrender demand from the German commander. His reply stunned the Germans and became a sensational morale boost for the troops at Bastogne and beyond. Instead of accepting the surrender demand and going into captivity for the remainder of the war, General McAuliffe said, "Nuts." The

Germans were perplexed and did not know what the comment meant. When informed, that loosely translated, it expressed, "Go to the devil," they stormed off in a fit of anger.

General McAuliffe listened to the inner voice that told him to refuse the perceived "easy way out" of surrender, and persevere with the faith that his allies would rescue his troops. He received his reward soon when the weather cleared, and American planes resupplied his unit. Good fortune continued when the 101st Airborne and defenders of Bastogne were reinforced a few days later and repelled the German offensive. Five months later, the war in Europe was over.

Pressure affects everything and everyone differently, and at different times of our lives. We all experience a mixture of good and bad choices, successes, and failures, and I am no exception.

Opportunities for great success and troubles can lead to dramatic failures. Both come with pressure. By themselves, neither result is inevitable, but our responses and the activities resulting from choosing a path influence the results.

Pressure makes us look for a quick and easy way out to resume a comfortable and peaceful course in life. I've learned "the easy way out" is seldom easy and less frequently the way out of any challenge.

Often the right choice is the one that is more difficult to make and challenging to execute, but leads to more success and a subsequent path going forward.

What experiences have put you under pressure? Do you have a mixture of results that have prepared you for your next pressure-packed decision? Are you better able to assist those in your sphere of influence when they experience pressure because of your experiences?

SECTION FOUR
SAFE HARBOR AHEAD!

Hope and Optimism

Love Overcomes All Things

Have you seen love overcome the greatest of obstacles and challenges lately? Did you pause and bask in its magnificence?

The ancient Roman poet Virgil wrote, "Love Overcomes All Things," which people have quoted over the millennia.

I know it sounds trite, but if ever there was a time that idiom fit, it is with this story. It began for me on a Saturday morning after my daughter Elizabeth's high school softball game in 2015. She awoke to find someone egged the house.

Her mother quickly located the carton, determined where the eggs came from and scurried to the store to find the culprits. We suspected it might have been a prank pulled by some of her teammates. They called me to come over to dispatch the mess before it became intolerable.

The store video clearly showed three girls leaving the store with the eggs, and they were students at a rival high school. Elizabeth didn't know them. What was their motive?

Ultimately it was determined one of the girls named Annie was made jealous of Elizabeth by a boy because Elizabeth had gone to homecoming with him. Since the boy was on the football team, they only spent about an hour together at Whataburger after the game. Elizabeth had not gone out with him again.

The offenders were confronted and warned not to misbehave again. Things calmed down, and I thought the experience would reside in the memory bank of our lives.

Some months later, I learned Annie was expecting a baby by that boy. I was surprised to learn Elizabeth had become friends with her as well.

Annie could have taken the "easy way out" and had a medical procedure to dispose of the "problem." That choice would have made her life easier for the moment and enabled her to enjoy all of the temporal pleasures of high school and college life. The boy and his family wanted nothing to do with the child. Thankfully, Annie determined to have the baby and her family and friends completely supported her decision.

In March of 2016, Braelynn, or as we call her B, was born. Annie brought B to Elizabeth's high school softball games early and often. You could see her devotion to B in her every action.

I have to say B is one of the cutest little girls I have ever seen. There is no way to know presently of the impact she and her descendants will have on this world. But one thing is sure. If she weren't born, we today, and people in the future would be the biggest losers.

Annie continued her education as a health care administration student while dedicated to B's upbringing. Faithful to provide for our every need, God sent Justin into her and B's life, and they were married in the summer of 2020. Elizabeth was blessed to be in the wedding party.

I believe Annie will impact countless numbers of people in her life as well. However, if she doesn't do anything except being a wonderful mother to B, she will be a hero to many.

I'm grateful Elizabeth had the open heart to meet and befriend Annie after their unusual introduction. Elizabeth's life is forever changed, and for the better. They both had to become more mature people to overcome the initial incident and discover true friendship.

Annie has already impacted my life as well and taught me the Bible verse in John 15:13, "**Greater love hath no man than this, that a man lay down his life for his friends**" doesn't absolutely require you have to die for someone to fulfill it. Annie lives that verse every day, and is a walking testimonial of the value of friendship, life, and unconditional love.

In this world of negativity and evil, we all need to recognize and celebrate people like Annie. And, we need to cherish and nurture the Braelynn's of the world! When we do so, our spirits will rise, and we will receive the inspiration to live better lives as well.

When is the last time you saw love conquer all? Will you be more vigilant looking for it in your life and surroundings?

The Dear John Message
that Will Lift Every Heart

My son John was born when I was forty-five years old. I was concerned about living long enough to teach him the important things in life. It was important to me for him to benefit from the lessons I had learned, without making the mistakes I had made.

When he was six months old, I wrote the following letter and filed it in case something happened to me.

Unfortunately, we lost John in 1998 before I had the opportunity to teach him these lessons. I included this letter in *Surviving Grief by God's Grace* in 2002 and offer it to you with the prayer you may find something here to benefit you and your family.

I believe its message is as pertinent in today's environment as the day I wrote it.

December 17, 1997

My dearest John-

The following are things I hope to teach you early in life to make you happy, more successful, and richer in spirit. If I pass away before I'm able to personally teach you these things, I truly hope you will take them to heart. I love you very much and I wish the best for you. I want you to fly the highest, achieve your dreams, and positively impact others' lives. All the while, I hope you will also experience the least amount of unhappiness.

I love you,

Dad

1. God exists. Have faith, pray, and listen.
2. Love and care for your mother. You will be the man of the house. She unconditionally loves you and deserves your love, respect, and attention.
3. Learn early, learn often; never stop learning. It will determine the level of your success.
4. Remember: You learn more from your mistakes than your successes.
5. ALWAYS have a positive attitude.
6. Don't speak ill of others.

7. Don't listen to negativism. It is a cancer that will deter you from success.
8. SMILE. Say please and thank you.
9. Be sincere.
10. Be on time!
11. Be humble.
12. Keep your word.
13. Be proactive.
14. You will make mistakes. Don't be afraid. It's not how many times you get knocked down in life that counts, but how many times you get back up.
15. "Can't" never did anything. This is from your Papaw Battle.
16. There is ALWAYS an alternative choice.
17. You don't have to know everything, but you do have to know enough to keep from being taken advantage of. Another gem from your Papaw Battle.
18. You are no better and no worse than anyone else.
19. Be VERY grateful for what you have. It doesn't take long to find someone worse off than you are.
20. Have a sense of humor. Things are never as bad as they may appear. A sense of humor will lighten most situations.
21. Anyone can do the things they like. Those who do the things they must do, but don't want to, will have greater success than the majority.
22. The "easy way out" is usually only easy in the short run.
23. Think before you act.
24. There are consequences to your actions (choices and decisions).

25. Beware of the unintended consequences of your actions.
26. Watch your expectations of others. They are only human and will let you down if you expect them to be perfect.
27. If you want to receive loyalty, you must first be loyal to others.
28. Be considerate of others with your actions.
29. Treat other people's property as you want others to treat yours.
30. Just because someone has something you don't have doesn't mean they are rich.
31. Even if they are rich, it is no excuse for abusing them or their property.
32. Be patient. Nothing is free, and you have to pay dues to reap the rewards in life.
33. Most rich and successful people paid their dues. Learn from them, but don't envy them.
34. Feelings of anger and envy don't hurt the other person half as much as they hurt you because they prevent you from focusing and achieving positive results.
35. Strive for excellence in ALL things.
36. To be an effective leader, you must also be a good follower.
37. Be honest. ALWAYS tell the truth. People will forgive a mistake, but will never trust a liar.
38. What you think is what you feel. THINK POSITIVE!
39. Revere the past. The wisdom of the ages is at your fingertips.
40. There are two types of people. Those who look for ways to make things happen, and those who look for

reasons why things can't happen. They both achieve what they see.

41. Former coach of the Carolina Panthers, Dom Capers, has a great philosophy. It is:

    Expect Nothing

    Work Hard

    Prepare for the worst

    Hope for the best

42. Be creative. Always be thinking of ways to improve yourself and/or the things you're doing.

43. Make friends with as many people as possible. Those relationships are the most important thing in life next to your relationship with God and your family. If you have friends and you are a true friend in return, you will be able to have a wide range of opportunities during your life.

God bless Texas! God bless the USA! We are blessed by being able to live in the greatest area in the world. This country doesn't owe you anything. If you want something, be prepared to earn it.

Forrest Gump's Mama was Right

Have you ever recounted how many unusual events you have experienced that you couldn't possibly have planned to happen?

Merriam-Webster's on-line dictionary defines the word "serendipity" as, "the faculty or phenomenon of finding valuable or agreeable things not sought for." That is the definition of what I'm discussing, but I like a more down-to-earth illustration.

The movie *Forrest Gump* won the 1994 Best Picture Academy Award and five other Oscars. Forrest repeatedly relates to the endless stream of people who spend time with him on a bench waiting for his bus that his mama always told him, "Life is like a box of chocolates. You never know what you're going to get." He then illustrates the advice with examples from his unique life experiences.

While most of us haven't experienced everything Forrest did, I'll bet you would be amazed at the list of your unique experiences.

I have written elsewhere about some of the unpleasant, challenging, gut punches along my path. I would like to illustrate Forrest's point with a couple of positive surprises I realized.

My friends Doyle, John, and I would travel to the Cotton Bowl in Dallas while we were in college to "scalp" football tickets for the Dallas Cowboys games. Yes, the Cowboys originally played in the Cotton Bowl before Texas Stadium and AT&T Stadium, (or Jerry's World as it is affectionately known).

We thought of the idea to attend games inexpensively and/or make a few dollars for fun from Doyle's father, who we knew as Babe. Babe taught us the techniques that made us successful and provided us a lot of fun at the same time.

Sometimes we would obtain tickets and go to a game. On other times we would secure tickets and pocket a few extra dollars, and occasionally we would earn some dollars and leave for other locations in search of entertainment.

In August of 1970 or 1971, we ventured down to the State of Texas fairgrounds, where the Cowboys were going to play a Saturday evening pre-season game. I took up position on the steps leading to gate A, which is the main gate, and Doyle and John fanned out looking for money–making opportunities.

We didn't see the game that night. Because of what happened next, I also forgot how much money we may have made.

As I stood on the steps rising toward the gate, I surveyed the landscape looking for someone to buy the tickets I was holding, or someone who might desire to sell their extra tickets.

In those days, the lane containing the Midway was a street used by vehicles when the State Fair wasn't in operation. There wasn't any traffic on the road (that I remember) until a long black limousine pulled up and stopped in front of the gate.

The driver exited the vehicle and opened the door allowing the passenger could climb out of the back seat. Because of the lack of other activities, I found myself watching with interest for a possible ticket customer. To my surprise, the most famous actor from my lifetime, John Wayne, stood up and stretched his six-foot four frame and began walking toward the gate where I stood. I realized I didn't have a pen and paper and certainly didn't have a camera. As he strode in his unique and famous fashion ever closer to me, my mind raced on what to do.

Finally, he stepped in front of me, and instinctively I extended my hand to shake his. He reached out and shook my hand. He complimented the handshake with the broad smile that was also a trademark in his movies. I asked him, "Would you like to buy any tickets"? He replied, "No, thank you," released my hand, and continued walking into the stadium. I stood there in disbelief with what had just happened.

Doyle and John returned to the steps to ask me the details of the too-brief encounter. They are the only witnesses to the event for which I'm grateful. Otherwise, it would be easy for me to wonder if it really happened.

I couldn't wait to return home and tell the story to my mother because she was a bigger John Wayne fan than I was. As expected, she was excited about my good fortune.

The second example occurred on April 3rd, 1991 when I worked with one of my sales reps in Tampa. Because I love baseball, I asked him if there were any spring training games we could attend during my trip.

He discovered the Cincinnati Reds were playing the Detroit Tigers that evening at the stadium now known as Publix Field at Joker Marchant Stadium. I asked him if we needed to pre-buy tickets, and he said obtaining seats would not be a challenge.

We drove to Lakeland shortly before game time and were startled when we arrived at the stadium. It appeared the stands were full, and there must have been a line of two to three hundred people desiring to buy tickets. We were dumbfounded at why this was occurring for a weeknight pre-season baseball game in an area where games happened daily, and there was more than one team holding their pre-season training camp and games in the area.

Instead of walking to the back-of-the-line, we sought out ticket sellers who were eager to turn their tickets into a quick profit.

RICHARD V. BATTLE

We paid $ 20 each for seats whose face value was significantly less than $10.

We reached our seats and joined the crowd in enjoying the game on a rare evening with low humidity in Florida. Inning after inning, the game progressed without revealing anything justifying the crowd size or ticket prices. Then it happened. The Tigers were batting in the bottom of the eighth. The stadium announcer in his rich baritone voice stated, "Now batting for the Tigers, pinch-hitter, Tom Selleck."

We were stunned. The crowd of 7,200 erupted with appreciation and enthusiasm, unlike experienced by most players and even fewer pinch-hitters. We learned Selleck's appearance was written about in the local paper before the game, which explained the large and energetic crowd. Unfortunately for the Tigers and their fans, Tom Selleck struck out on six pitches after two foul balls, and the Tigers lost the game 6-4.

In addition to the unexpected good fortune of watching Tom Selleck, I was able to see the longest home run I ever witnessed by Cecil Fielder for the Tigers that evening.

So the next time something provides you a surprise, remember Forrest Gump's mama and her box of chocolates explanation of serendipity.

What You Do When You Get Out of a Hole Is More Important Than How You Got into It!

When was the last time you found yourself in a hole with no perceived way out? How did you eventually make it out? Did you resume your previous course, or begin a new path? Can you look back and appreciate the lessons learned that improved your life?

We can all find ourselves in a hole multiple times in our lives. Sometimes our actions caused our challenge, and sometimes circumstances occurred beyond our view and control.

Regardless, what we do once we find ourselves in the hole is what differentiates each of us in the resulting path moving forward. Can we extricate ourselves? Do we need assistance? Do we have to compromise our values?

The first time I can remember being in a literal hole, I was about four or five years old. I was with my grandfather at the feed store. He was there for serious business, and I was there to get into trouble like any good young boy.

The next thing you know, I'm in a hole deeper than my height in the hopper for the feed grinder. I could not climb out of to escape on my own. It burned such an impression into my mind I can still envision that day, the store, and my trap.

I remember calling for help, and fortunately, my grandfather overcame his embarrassment and rescued me before the whole town of Commerce, Texas heard my cries. Once I was asleep that evening, I'm sure my grandparents shared a good laugh over the entire episode.

How we respond to the adversities or holes we experience will reshape our life's journey. Whether we escape a hole ourselves or with assistance, our attitude will determine whether we turn the event into a positive contributor to our lives, or an impediment. If we focus on how we arrived in a hole, we will entrap ourselves and restrict our growth. If we learn the lessons from the unpleasant experience and apply them as we proceed toward our goals, we will realize a much fuller life.

I wrote this brief piece below that encapsulate the effects of adversity on man.

The Frailty of Man
Pressure that results from adversity reveals our character.
We all fail under pressure some of the time;
Some of us fail under pressure all of the time.
Thankfully, we all don't fail under pressure all of the time;
Those successes under pressure build our society and forge progress.

My long-time friend, Dr. George Lowe, is inspirational to me. We have belonged to the same church for many years and share a love for all Texas Longhorns sports.

George is a brilliant man who was a leading cardiologist in Austin, Texas, for many years. He is worthy of admiration for that accomplishment alone. His modesty limits the number of people who learn his story of becoming a doctor, which is phenomenal and encouraging to anyone who finds themselves in a hole or facing adversity.

Upon graduation from The University of Texas at Austin, George accepted a job with Humble Oil (now Exxon) in Baytown,

Texas. During his performance review after his second year, it became apparent to everyone his progress was insufficient. As Will Rogers said, "If you find yourself in a hole, stop digging." George decided to stop digging the hole he was in as a chemical engineer.

Instead of responding negatively, blaming others, and masking the disappointment with destructive behavior, George resumed his studies in Austin, hoping to find his purpose in life.

A friend from his undergraduate days, Webb Ashley, asked George to tutor him in quantitative analysis so he could attend medical school. A passing statement from Webb that George should attend med school planted a seed into his sub-conscious. A week later, he happened to see a sign about the Medical College Admission Test (MCAT), which is a requirement for acceptance to medical school, and he registered for the test.

George studied twelve hours a day for six weeks and he prayed. He overcame a stutter that could have derailed med school, passed the interview, and spent the next eight years excelling at all of the requirements, finishing first in the National Board Exam. In his fifty-year career, he performed 11,000 triumphant procedures as a cardiologist.

Imagine how many lives Dr. George Lowe improved directly and indirectly because he didn't allow that one hole, or any other, to define his life. Said differently by my friend J. Terryl "Bubba" Bechtol, "The secret of success in life is not how many times that you get knocked down, but how many times that you get back up." Boy, did George Lowe get back up!

Webb Ashley, who never went to medical school, made what seemed to be an inadvertent comment that sparked an inspiration and contributed to an unimaginable number of lives. As I have written before, encouragement is the greatest gift we can give almost everyone.

Looking back, I can see people who influenced my life like Webb Ashley, and I would wager you can also.

How Can Our Time in a Hole Benefit our Future?

- **Will Rogers warning to stop digging when you're in a hole and compounding a problem is still valid.**
- **We only fail when we quit. Until then, there is always an opportunity to turn failure into success.**
- **Many times, our journey leads us to a different destination than we planned.**
- **We never know the number of people or the amount of impact we may have with a timely word of encouragement to others.**

Hopefully, we learn from each hole we fall into, and find ourselves in fewer of them as we proceed down life's path. How can we also listen and learn from others to respond to our challenges in a way that most benefits us, and others whose lives we touch?

THE 2020 v2.0 AND
BEYOND OFFICIAL WHAT'S
IN AND OUT LIST!

Have you ever desired the reboot of a year with the hope of avoiding a cataclysmic event?

The COVID-19 pandemic, like most trials, produced some positive changes in people's lives as well as the more visible and publicized negative ones. Those shifts reminded me of the annual in-and-out of style lists published in newspapers such as *The Washington Post* and *Seattle Times* at the beginning of each new year.

In our more stable lives before the spring of 2020, the in-style choices were usually light-weight and shallow. Even the out-of-style choices often focused on unimportant alternatives. The stories were entertaining and good conversation starters but influenced very few people's daily lives.

In the spirit of rebooting a version 2.0 for 2020 and beyond, I believe a new list is warranted. I have created the "official" one for your review, enjoyment, and hopefully benefit below.

The *Official What's In and Out List for 2020* - **Version 2.0**

<u>Out</u>	<u>In</u>
Reliance on man	**Faith in God**
Materialism	**Spiritualism**
Fads	**Family and relationships**
Celebrity	**Real-life heroes**
Movie	Military
Television	Firefighters
Career Politicians	Citizen governance
Media	First responders
Pundits	Medical professionals
Commentators	Farmers and ranchers
Internet	Grocers, restaurants
Reality (is there such a thing?)	Transportation
Musicians	Teachers

RICHARD V. BATTLE

Sports	Power, water, communication
Freeloaders	All who make our country work
Giving without discernment	Helping family, friends and neighbors in need
Climate change	Food, water, and shelter
Unproven theory	Proven, practical, common sense
Superficial	Substantive
Frivolous	Serious
Fantasy	Reality
Surface Swimming (Shallow)	Critical thinking
Entitled	Opportunity
Orwellian	Freedom
Government provision	Liberty
Executive orders	Representative republic legislation
Bad cops	Good cops
Hyphenated Americans	Americans

So-called celebrities tell us how to live if they aren't busy revealing sensational stories about themselves to maintain their market value and presence on the public stage. In prosperous times, they may find a larger audience than during difficult days where we value the advice of people who can assist us in navigating unpleasant reality.

Advocacy groups for every cause you can think of barrage us with messages that civilization will end if we don't submit to their demands and sacrifice our liberty and financial resources. When our leisure time is plentiful, and our pockets are full of money, it is easy to become bored and prey for campaigns appealing to us, to impulsively trade our assets to fund their endeavors. When the chips are down, our eyesight is laser-focused on what is most important, and our susceptibility to emotional appeals decreases.

History has repeatedly demonstrated that rent-a-mobs generally appear during prosperity, but fade away when people are focused on the essentials of life.

In plentiful times, a problem we experience can be too many choices in nearly every area of life. It is a blessing of the free enterprise system often overlooked.

Our parents and grandparents, who endured the great depression and World War II, couldn't imagine the grandeur so frequently taken for granted in the current generation. They prioritized need over luxury and endured deprivation and sacrifice to gift us a land of plenty and leisure. We Americans have been blessed because of the efforts of our forefathers.

The COVID-19 pandemic has given us a small glimpse of what others have faced more universally with shortages of toilet paper and hand sanitizer as examples.

My desire would be for our country to experience peace and prosperity continually but retain the common-sense values that sustain and enable us to navigate the dark days of despair that occasionally appear in our lives.

How would you reboot a year? What things would you discard? What would you prioritize? What would your "in-and-out" list look like? Is there any reason not to reorder your choices now and on an on-going basis?

Resilient, Recommitted, Refocused, Reenergized, Relentless and Resolved!

Not since World War II has the United States been threatened as we are now with the COVID-19 pandemic of 2020.

On the surface, the menace appeared only to touch people's physical health, but it didn't take long to see that a greater peril more broadly attacked all of us.

The spring of 2020 brought a global health pandemic not seen since the Spanish flu in 1918-1920. Many felt like one month lasted an eternity, and the year was even longer.

The unprecedented shuttering of the country to "flatten the curve" of hospital admissions produced the unintended consequences of financially threatening the destruction of the medical industry. Most other services were suspended, which resulted in massive layoffs when COVID cases were less than anticipated.

The uncertainty and loss of control increased people's anxiety levels. Governments forced travel restrictions, closed businesses, and added unwelcome pressures to virtually everyone's lives. The first order of the day was to be **resilient** to the attack individually and as a nation.

It presented us with an excellent opportunity to visualize what was important in life and a priority compared to things that were luxuries or insignificant.

We have also seen, unsurpassed in our 240 plus year history, power grabs by politicians of all parties and at all levels of government in 2020. The precedent and future possibilities that may come to pass because of this unchallenged seizure of power is breathtaking!

The time is now for all of us to **recommit** to the words of Abraham Lincoln. He dedicated the military cemetery at Gettysburg on November 19, 1863. His statement, **"This nation, under God, shall have a new birth of freedom -- and that government of the people, by the people, for the people, shall not perish from the earth."**

Failure to solidly re-establish the Constitution, rule-of-law, and Representative Republic we inherited as our steadfast principles will lead to a further and eventual destruction of our government and way-of-life.

It is up to us to **refocus** and act to ensure the country that emerges from the pandemic is the one we want and expect to exist in the future. As the saying goes, "Failure to act, is acting to fail," and we will only realize the amount of liberty from power-hungry politicians we demand.

How can we refocus our lives and find more fulfillment?

- **Deepen our faith.**
- **Enhance our relationships with family and friends.**
- **Realize no government can protect us from the risks of life.**
- **Realize no government cares about us as individuals.**
- **Realize climate, weather, and disease models are no better than the data supplied and the biases of those submitting the data.**
- **Be grateful for our fellow men and women who work hard every day to offer those things in exchange that we can't as efficiently supply ourselves.**
- **It is our responsibility to remind and demand government officials they work for "we the people," not the other way around.**

How will we respond to current events threatening our physical, mental, spiritual, and financial health? Each of us must **reenergize** ourselves to defend and continue to build our great country.

We can pay the price by contributing to our country to continue its success, or pay the price because we have failed to do so. Our duty to our family, our country, and ourselves is to be **relentless** in our efforts and unwavering in our resolve to leave this life with no regrets!

We are free to choose what price we want to pay, but we all benefit or suffer the results.

What choice will you make today to improve the trajectory of your life's journey?

A Dream Delayed is Not a Dream Denied

What great dream have you delayed by other choices or circumstances beyond your control?

Too often, we fear a dream *withheld* to us, for one reason or another, will be *denied* to us for a lifetime. It does not have to be that way.

There are many examples from my personal experience, the experiences of those whom I know, and even examples from public figures. I hope you will visualize that sometimes the delay is beneficial for us and all whom we may touch when the dream finally is fulfilled.

I attended a personal development course required by my company in 2002. The homework assignment for the next class was to write about one lesson I learned from my first job.

That evening, I couldn't sleep. The many lessons I learned as an eleven-year-old paperboy overcame me. Ideas raced through my mind. I wrote fourteen lessons I learned in a notebook so I wouldn't forget them. Since I was in the process of publicly sharing the experience of losing my son through *Surviving Grief by God's Grace*, I filed the piece of paper. Little did I know what would happen to it.

Four years later, time and space crossed paths. I stumbled across the paper while rummaging through my desk. When I reviewed what I had written down, I realized the lessons had been life-altering and positively impacted nearly every facet of my life. Feeling the need to share my awakening with others, I wrote *The Four-Letter Word that Builds Character.*

So many people have shared with me their appreciation for the influence of that book on their lives. Those affirmations of my experience and undertaking continually inspire my efforts to positively impact others.

I received the gift of the experience and story, but initiative and persistence were required to finish the book. Both characteristics demanded a positive attitude to overcome the foreboding that the time for the dream of telling the story had passed.

There are many other examples, but I want to share two with you. The first is someone I know personally, and the other is one well known worldwide by first name only.

I met Jenine Lori at the 2019 Readers Favorite book award ceremony in Miami, Florida. She won the Bronze Medal for Children's – Religious Theme books for *Surprise, I have 3 Eyes!*

As Jenine and I discussed our books and the wonderful event **Readers Favorite** hosted to celebrate them, she shared that her book was the result of a twelve-year-old dream. I was fascinated with her story and impressed, as it made my four-year journey with *The Four-Letter Word that Builds Character* seem puny.

Below is her summary and the tremendous example of perseverance:

"In 2005, I was newly married and thinking of starting a family. I had been a teacher and visual artist but never considered writing. As I waited in the car to pick up my mother-in-law, rhythmical sentences began flooding my mind with powerful messages. I grabbed a notebook and wrote what was came to me filling it in no time. Later, I shared my stories with others who agreed they were destined to be children's books.

I read the stories to my stepson, who loved their enchantment. Encouraged by the reception of the stories, and after months of research, I submitted my manuscript to several publishing companies and waited. Time past and I heard nothing. Months became years and the birth of a child took precedence in my life. The stories were forgotten.

Ten years later, I was going through a challenging process and began to question things. I felt unfulfilled and desired to live a more fulfilling life with a higher purpose. I wanted to contribute more to others, which would provide me immense joy.

Remembering the stories I had written years before, I relocated the manuscript and cried when I reread it. The stories were as magical as I remembered. I knew my new purpose was to write consciousness-raising awareness books for children!

Inspired to seize the moment, I authored, illustrated, and independently published my first children's book, **_Surprise; I have 3 eyes!_** two years later.

It became a #1 international bestseller, won numerous international book awards and was featured as the #1 book in the U.K. for children with special needs. It continues reaching around the world inspiring uniqueness, creativity, and the belief anything is possible!

The moral my story is: "**When we dream, believe in life's magic, and trust our ability to make our dreams a reality, everything and anything is possible!**"

I met so many astonishing people at the event. My appreciation, respect, and admiration for their creativity, dedication, and effort grew exponentially.

RICHARD V. BATTLE

Few had ever heard the name of Daniel Ruettiger, except for Notre Dame football fans, when the movie *Rudy* burst onto the scene in the fall of 1993. His life-long dream was to play football for Notre Dame, but everyone and everything told him he would never fulfill his dream. He was too small, too slow, and an average student.

If he listened to the voices, few beyond his family and friends would know of him and receive inspiration from his incredible journey and accomplishment. It is a true story that is stranger than fiction.

Now recognizable throughout the world by his nickname, **Rudy,** he shares his story of persistence, patience, grit, determination, intrepidness, and a never-quit attitude as a public speaker to inspire others to relentlessly pursue their dreams. The road he successfully navigated to reach this point is beyond belief.

Dyslexia impaired his formal studies, and he joined the United States Navy upon his high school graduation. After a two-year hitch, he spent the next two years working in an industrial plant. When others would discard their dream, Rudy maintained his, despite others calling him foolish to do so.

Since he didn't qualify academically for Notre Dame, he first entered Holy Cross College to prove he could complete college-level academic work and raise his grades. After two years and three rejections, he gained acceptance to his beloved Notre Dame.

Six years removed from high school, Rudy was finally a student at Notre Dame and earnestly began his pursuit as a walk-on football player. Overcoming financial challenges by working on campus, and his small stature with dogged determination, he was finally rewarded to play, for the last game in 1975.

History records his twenty-seven seconds of playtime, including sacking the opposing quarterback, which created such excitement he rode off of the field on the shoulders of his teammates.

We will never achieve all of our dreams, but that realization is no reason not to pursue your dreams until their achievement, or we until leave this earth. Even if we don't achieve a dream, it is almost a certainty that we will accomplish more than if we never pursued the goal at all.

Two quotes I find encouraging are:

"Don't quit until every base is uphill." – Babe Ruth

"It is better to aim at the sky and strike an eagle than to aim at the eagle and strike a rock." – Native American proverb

What great dream do you hold deep inside your soul? Is it one you have regarded in the past tense because you have relegated it as unachievable? How will your mood and actions change if you acknowledge, until your life is over, that you still may achieve it? What can you do today to rekindle it and keep its embers burning until the day you can celebrate its achievement?

My desire is for each of you to experience the awakening of your dreams, and to realize your life's journey is more fruitful in their pursuit.

Don't Allow Yourself to be Pigeon-holed!

Have you ever noticed a surprised look from your family, friends, co-workers, supervisors, or others when you accomplished something outside of their perception of you? Were you astonished, happy, or sad when you recognized it occurring to you?

It is common for people to only see us as a person in the singular role they encounter us. It is much rarer to be viewed for our future potential rather than our present and past status.

It is a frequent conversation starter when meeting someone new to ask, "What do you do?" That question has always troubled me because I have a wide variety of experiences, thereby defying a simple answer. It reminds me of the party question from years ago, "What's your sign?" I became so annoyed with that shallow inquiry my standard reply was, "No right turn on red." Some people laughed, others thought I was crazy, and the remainder did both. My belief is **what you do, is not who you are**. I prefer asking a broader question to gain a detailed answer to what someone is interested in and the many ways they exercise their interest.

One example I quickly observed in volunteer organizations was how people were assigned responsibilities. Members expected accountants to serve as treasurers, salespeople to fundraise, and ladies to serve as the secretary. One of the benefits of volunteering is the opportunity to serve in areas other than your professional expertise to improve your skills to broaden and enhance your career. I enjoyed gaining accounting, legal, publicity, and other skills that benefitted me in my profession.

After I left a long corporate career, I encountered several people who were surprised not only with my new activities but some they were even unaware of from previous years.

When I announced the publication of my sixth book, ***Conquering Life's Course: Common Sense in Chaotic Times*** in 2019, I

RICHARD V. BATTLE

had more than one-person state they were unaware I had even written one book. I found those remarks amusing as I published *The Volunteer Handbook: How to Organize and Manage a Successful Organization* in 1988!

My book marketing efforts were ineffective!

Others were surprised to learn of my long experience as a public speaker because it was outside of my relationship with them.

If we want to be more, we have to do more, but we also need to have our friends see what we're doing so we can be better servants for others, and they may be able to help us be more successful in our other efforts.

If we allow others to see us in only one way, it will only limit the impact of our endeavors.

An example is Dan Marcinek, a friend from church, who left a successful career in the construction industry and became a nurse.

Dan still loves building and continues to exercise that passion with the church mission team. However, his desire to help people led him to make a change beyond most people's perception of "what he does."

His pivotal moment came as he returned home from work one day. He stopped to help a stranger replace a flat tire, and the feeling he received from helping others overwhelmed him. A combination of timing and his new revelation led him to resume his college studies. His interest in science guided him into the field of nursing, which also enabled him to help others.

While still working to provide for his family, Dan spent eight years in school to earn his registered nurse (RN) certification. He overcame an exceedingly frustrating setback, which could have provided him an excuse for abandoning his quest. His love of science, stubbornness, and refusal to quit exceeded his obstacles. So he persisted and succeeded.

As of this writing, Dan is enjoying working with patients and his co-workers. His life experiences provide him an additional opportunity to help others. He is continuing his educational efforts and hopes to eventually earn a master's degree and teach, which would expand his mission to serve.

Dan is a tremendous example of someone who answered a call to be more, overcame many forms of resistance to achieve his goal, and is still laboring to improve himself. His efforts focus on positively impacting the lives of more people.

Another terrific and inspiring example is Michael Atkins. His progression in the Denver school system from a student, part-time and then full-time custodian, para-professional, assistant principal, and finally principal is spectacular.

His story is noteworthy for several reasons. First, he proves the value of honest work at any level. Second, when others showed Michael he could become more, he overcame any fear to work toward his goal. Third, he overcame any racial obstacles and hardships others may have used to discontinue their effort. Finally, he recognizes his example and its value in helping countless others to reach for their dreams.

Michael Atkins did not allow others to define who he was or would be. He shares the lesson his grandmother told him, "It is important to **write your own story.**" How wise his grandmother was! Who knows how many people may benefit because of his actions in the future?

We are not limited in our opportunities in The United States, unlike other countries. Everyone in the US can aspire to pursue their dreams and happiness at whatever time and in the manner they desire. No one is guaranteed success, and most of the people we admire for their achievements tell stories of overcoming multiple hardships and challenges, but success is still achievable if we are willing to work for it.

How Can We Achieve More and avoid being pigeon-holed?

- **Be a life-long learner.**
- **Stretch yourself with roles outside of your area of expertise.**
- **If you want to be more, do more.**

- **Learn from failure to increase your confidence and competence.**
- **Inform others of your accomplishments not to brag, but to enable them to see your potential.**
- **As Michael Atkins says, "Write your own story!"**
- **Aim High, Work Hard, NEVER quit!**

If you're happy where you are, this story may not appeal to you. But I hope you won't discount it too quickly. If you only inspire your children or grandchildren, as Michael Atkins grandmother did, you will provide a gift of immeasurable value to your family's future.

If you desire more, I hope this will inspire you to "**aim high, work hard and NEVER quit**" in your drive to reach for your dreams.

None of us know if we will achieve everything we attempt, but it is a certainty we will achieve much more if we persist and strain in the effort until our last breath.

My desire is for you to periodically look back during your journey and find amazement at more achievements than you ever dreamed possible. My hope is you turn that astonishment into fuel to accelerate yourself further and faster to your ultimate desired destination.

Run Through the Tape!

Have you ever had others get ahead of you?

With the end of the year in sight, successful people tend to relax and enjoy the fruits of their labor. They feel they can start up again at the start of the New Year and want to be well rested.

That kind of thinking is dangerous for the individual and organization. For once the exertion of effort necessary to be successful is withdrawn, it is never as easy to resume the activity or realize the same level of success. I have seen individuals, organizations, and businesses suffer the consequences from this, despite applying every known technique.

The primary analogy I want to use to explain this phenomenon is a track race. Regardless of distance, every race begins with a burst of energy, and then the racers implement their strategies for winning. Often, the person who takes the lead and sets the pace doesn't end up winning the race.

At the finish line of every race, a ribbon-like tape is stretched across the track, approximately chest high. Every runner knows whomever reaches the tape first is the victor.

What happens if the leading runner slows down to hit the tape first, but doesn't plan on going past it? Many times this results in another racer passing the leader because he doesn't slow down his efforts until after he has run through the tape. The similarity between track and business is the worker who slows down at the end of the year. He plans to renew his effort at the beginning of the next year or race.

In track, coaches instruct every runner to focus, concentrate, and race all out until they have run *through* the tape. Only then is it acceptable to slow down to determine whether or not they were victorious. In the business world, people who run through the tape will not only succeed more in the current year, but also position themselves better to begin the New Year on a path to success. They reveal themselves to management as exceptional employees.

For those in sales, it is always more difficult to begin creating a new pipeline of prospective customers than it is to work an existing pipeline. Running through the tape provides that existing pipeline of prospects for the sales rep to begin their New Year successfully.

Even if you're not in sales or in a business that directly rewards production, the principle applies. As previously stated, but worthy of additional emphasis; the employee who maintains their successful habits is a team player and helps the business by running through the tape with their efforts all year long will be highly valued in any organization.

Whatever your endeavor is, I encourage you always give your best effort. Don't let the habits of others deter you from focusing your energy on accomplishing your goal or dream. Despite the adversity or setbacks you experience, NEVER QUIT until you break the tape, and win the race.

Can you see yourself winning more often than before?

Broadening our Shoulders for Those Coming Behind Us

What are we supposed to do once we have successfully traversed all the hazards of life and see safe harbor ahead?

Is it a time to relax and go away, or share the lessons learned from our long journey to make the trip easier for others?

We stand on the broad shoulders of giants who have gone before us. Knowingly or not, their efforts smoothed the way for our trip through life.

An adage that exists in many different versions says experience is the best teacher. Metaphorically, our predecessors explored and documented minefields, swift currents, treacherous whirlpools, and rapidly changing weather. It is our blessing to have access to their experience to learn the lessons they paid for, often with their lives.

For most generations until now, older relatives were valued for their wisdom and advice. I wish I had proactively learned more from my relatives earlier, but I am glad I noted what I did. It has smoothed a trip marked with periodic challenges and enabled me to see my harbor in the distance.

Now, it is my turn to decide what I do with my broad and deep, successful, and unsuccessful experiences. Yes, I have the opportunity to enjoy many things that I deferred during my most active business years. However, I feel a responsibility to **return the favor** to those I knew and others that I do not know. They delivered to me a life with a big opportunity and more ease than in other times and places.

My hope is that everyone arrives at a point in their journey to consider how they might impact our future descendants and the world they will inhabit. There is no definitive method for us to follow. Each of us is blessed with unique gifts and talents, enabling us to impact the coming world positively.

Evidence of a failure to instill an appreciation for the positive contributions of our past to our present abounds. Many young people ignore history or rely on social media in its place for guidance on daily living.

The cancel cultures' progress has accelerated in 2020 with the destruction of statues and monuments celebrating individuals and events. Ironically, in their haste to destroy virtually everything from the past, some heroes of causes supposedly advocated currently were removed as well.

Matthias Baldwin was a successful 19th-century industrialist most known for manufacturing locomotives. His faith inspired him to fund a school for African-American children in 1835 and advocate for their voting rights in 1837. He was active early in his efforts to abolish slavery. After his death, citizens erected a statue to him in Philadelphia in appreciation for his efforts to benefit those less fortunate than he was.

How much better would it be to celebrate Baldwin's example and teach current generations instead of in their ignorance of his endeavors destroying his statue?

Where will an embittered culture, with feelings of disdain and discrimination, travel? Will they triumph in throwing out the proven, successful parts of our civilization to install a society based on idealistic theories that have never succeeded anywhere in the world? While the utopian ideals advocated in academia sound ideal, they only work in a two-dimensional static format without real-world consequences. If only life were as simple as a classroom case study!

For our predecessors and ourselves, we have to make real-world decisions in a dynamic, three-dimensional arena with life-and-death, financial, and other consequences. In our daily lives, the data presented for decision is never complete and is always moving and changing. Failure hurts real people in every facet of their lives for varying lengths of time in the future.

Our choice is whether or not to proactively participate in defending what has worked, change what has impeded advancement, and share it using our gifts to help all in the future to enjoy a more fruitful life.

How can we reinstitute a contextual appreciation for the past to improve the future?

- **It is ok to enjoy the fruits of your labor.**
- **Resolve to contribute some of your time to share your experiences to help the future of others.**
- **Recognize there are generations without familial or formal educational awareness of the uniqueness of their country.**

- Instead of ceding the dialogue to the most angry and vocal voices: show-up, stand-up, and speak up to defend the best values of our society.
- Trumpet the imperfect, but advanced ideals of the American Revolution, and refuse to permit a revolution more resembling the French one in 1789.
- Communicate with those who only live for today based on morally fluid standards; the benefits of the accumulation of the development of our country.
- Relax and enjoy your safe harbor upon completion of your mission. Know your broadened shoulders, and the seed you planted will grow in the future and will benefit others.

Have you realized the importance of your life experiences? Have you discovered a market and method to share what you uniquely possess? Have you inspired others approaching their safe harbor to identify their opportunities to **return the favor to others**?

Notes

1. D'Sousa, Dinesh, Ronald Reagan: *How an Ordinary Man Became an Extraordinary Leader*, New York, *The Free Press*, 1997.

BIBLIOGRAPHY

Ambrose, Stephen E., *Undaunted Courage*, New York, Simon & Schuster, 1996.

Biography On-Line. www.biographyonline.net.

Covey, Stephen R., *The 7 Habits of Highly Effective People*, New York, Fireside, 1989.

Dixon, George, *War of the Worlds* radio broadcast causes chaos in 1938, New York Daily News, New York, New York, October 29, 2015 (Original publication October 31, 1938).

D'Sousa, Dinesh, Ronald Reagan: *How an Ordinary Man Became an Extraordinary Leader*, New York, *The Free Press*, 1997.

The Free Dictionary by Farlex on-line dictionary. http://www.thefreedictionary.com/.

Frink, Cheryl Coggins, *Keeping Faith, Austin American Statesman*, Austin, Texas, May 20, 1986.

Harris, Richard, *Reverisco, My Friend!*, *The Journal*, Buena Vista, Georgia, August 17, 2005.

Hsu, Benny, *Famous People Who Found Success Despite Failures, Get Busy Living* Podcast, May 26, 2011.

Lansing, Alfred, *Endurance: Shackleton's Incredible Voyage*, New York, Perseus Book Group, 1959.

Lossing, B. J., *Signers of the Declaration of Independence*, New York, Cooledge, 1848, reprinted 1995 by Wallbuilders Press as *The Lives of the Signers of the Declaration of Independence*.

Marey, Etienne-Jules, *Animal Mechanism: A Treatise on Terrestrial and Aerial Locomotion*, New York, D. Appleton, 1874.

McCullough, David, *The Wright Brothers*, New York, Simon and Schuster, 2015.

Merriam-Webster on-line dictionary, www.merriam-webster.com.

Miller, Diane Disney (As told to Pete Martin), *The Story of Walt Disney*, New York, Holt, 1957.

Powers, Kay, *Circus Veteran Ambitious at age 102, Austin American Statesman*, Austin, Texas, July 24, 1986.

Ramirez, Marc, *Polio Survivor Still Depends on Iron Lung, Dallas Morning News,* Dallas, Texas, May 25, 2018.

Selleck Strikes Out for Tigers, Chicago, *Chicago Tribune,* April 4, 1991.

Smith, Michael W., The Sacrifices Made By the Declaration Signers., http://michaelwsmith.com//2015/07/04//the-sacrifices-made-by-the-declaration-signers//July 4, 2015.

Tommy Morrissey: Showing the world that his limb difference makes no difference, Shriner's International, Tampa, Florida, 2016.

The Holy Bible, New International Version, **www.biblegateway. com.**

Wang, Dashun, *The Tipping Point Between Failure and Success, Harvard Business Review*, Boston, Massachusetts, 2019.

www.jenbricker.com.

www.Quotecounterquote.com.

www.youtube.com.

www.wikipedia.org.

Appendix A

Navigating Life's Journey **Quotations**

Smooth Sailing

"Stay away from negative people. They have a problem for every solution." – Albert Einstein

"Do what you can, with what you have, where you are at." – President Theodore Roosevelt

"To achieve all that is possible, we must attempt the impossible. To be as much as we can be, we must dream of being more." - Fred LaNovel

"The most important thing is faith in self and faith in God. Anything you can dream will come true." – Paul Alexander

"If not you, who? If not now, when? – President Ronald Reagan

"All the adversity I've had in my life, all my troubles and obstacles, have strengthened me... You may not realize it when it happens, but a kick in the teeth may be the best thing in the world for you." – Walt Disney

"But we are in the hands of a Higher Power, and puny mortals that we are, can do nothing to help ourselves against these colossal forces of nature." – Dr. Alexander H. Macklin, crew of Endurance

"A man who works for the immediate present and its immediate rewards is nothing but a fool."- Wilbur Wright

"Success is not final; failure is not fatal: it is the courage to continue that counts." – Winston Churchill

"When the storm clouds come, the eagle flies and the small birds run for cover." – Lewis Timberlake

"The secret of success in life is for a man to be ready for his opportunity when it comes." - Benjamin Disraeli

"Life's tragedy is that we get old too soon and wise too late." – Benjamin Franklin

"It is the greatest of all mistakes to do nothing when you can only do a little. Do what you can." – Sydney Smith

"A republic, if you can keep it." – Benjamin Franklin

"To be born free is an accident. To live free is a responsibility. But, to die free is an obligation." – John Ben Shepperd

The Water Around the Bend

"One person can make a difference and everyone should try."
- President John F. Kennedy

"The biggest lie in the world is a half-truth." – Bill Battle

"A lie can travel half way around the world while the truth is putting on its shoes." – Mark Twain

"Nothing great was ever achieved without enthusiasm." – Ralph Waldo Emerson

"Positive thinking is more than just a tagline. It changes the way we behave. And I firmly believe that when I am positive, it not only makes me better, but it also makes those around me better." – Harvey Mackay

"Can't never did anything." - Bill Battle

"NEVER say the word can't." – Sharon and Gerald Bricker

"If men were angels, no government would be necessary." – President James Madison

"Just when you thought it was safe to go back into the water." – Peter Benchley, *Jaws* 2

Troubled Water

"The difference between where you were yesterday and where you will be tomorrow lies in what you think and do today." - Claudia Tangerife Castillo

"**Those who do not learn history are doomed to repeat it**." – George Santayana and others

"Adapt, Improvise and Overcome." – Gunnery sergeant Tom Highway in *Heartbreak Ridge*

"Lord, let me save just one more." – Private Desmond Doss

"Nobody said it wasn't going to be semi-tough." – Billy Clyde Puckett in *Semi-Tough*

"Nuts!" – Brigadier General, Anthony McAuliffe, 101st Airborne Division

Safe Harbor Ahead!

"Love overcomes all things." – Virgil

"If you find yourself in a hole, stop digging." – Will Rogers

"The secret of success in life is not how many times that you get knocked down, but how many times that you get back up." – J. Terryl "Bubba" Bechtol

"When we dream, believe in life's magic, and trust our ability to make our dreams a reality, everything and anything is possible!" – Jenine Lori, Author

"Don't quit until every base is uphill." – Babe Ruth

"It is better to aim at the sky and strike an eagle, than to aim at the eagle and strike a rock." – Native American proverb

"Don't let someone write your story, make sure you write your own story," – Michael Atkins' grandmother

Additional Quotes

"Common sense is genius dressed in its working clothes." - Ralph Waldo Emerson

"There are no great men. There are only great challenges that ordinary men are forced by circumstances to meet." - Admiral William F. "Bull" Halsey Jr.

"Tolerance is the highest virtue for those who have no others." – G. K. Chesterton

"Success is getting what you want. Happiness is wanting what you get." – Comedian, Brother Dave Gardner

"Ah, but a man's reach should exceed his grasp. Or, what's a heaven for?" – Robert Browning

"When you come slam bang up against trouble, it never looks half as bad if you face up to it." - John Wayne

"No amount of evidence will ever persuade an idiot." – Mark Twain

"It's Always Too Soon to Quit." – Lewis Timberlake

"Youth, wasted on the young." – George Bernard Shaw

"Nothing in this world can take the place of persistence. Talent will not. Nothing is more common than unsuccessful people with talent. Genius will not. Unrewarded genius is almost a proverb. Education will not. The world is full of educated derelicts. Persistence and determination alone are omnipotent. The slogan 'Press On' has solved and always will solve the problems of the human race." – President Calvin Coolidge

"The greatest danger for most of us is not that our aim is too high and we miss it, but that it is too low and we reach it." – Michelangelo

"Never discourage anyone who continually makes progress, no matter how slow."– Plato

"If at first you don't succeed; try, try, again." – Popularized by William Edward Hickson

"It's better to light one candle than curse the darkness." – Chinese proverb

"The best executive is the one who has sense enough to pick good men (or women-RB) to do what he wants done, and self-restraint enough to keep from meddling with them while they do it." – President Theodore Roosevelt

"Service to humanity is the best work of life." – C. William Brownfield

"You can have anything you want in life if you just help enough other people get what they want." - Zig Ziglar

"When you're good to others, you're best to yourself." – Benjamin Franklin

"Gentlemen, we are going to relentlessly chase perfection, knowing full well we will not catch it, because nothing is perfect. But we're going to relentlessly chase it because in the process we will catch excellence. I am not interested in just being good." – Vince Lombardi

"Things may come to those who wait, but only the things left by those who hustle." — Abraham Lincoln

"Forget past mistakes. Forget failure. Forget everything except what you're going to do now and do it." William C. Durant

"Believe you can, and you're half way there." – President Theodore Roosevelt

"Never trouble trouble till trouble troubles you." - Unknown

"It's not what happens to you, but how you react to it that matters." — Epictetus

"Live simply, love generously, care deeply, speak kindly, leave the rest to God." – President Ronald Reagan

"In the middle of every difficulty, lies opportunity." – Albert Einstein

"We don't grow when things are easy. We grow when we face challenges." - Walexmarceva's Blog

"Much of the social history of the western world, over the past three decades, has been a history of replacing what worked for what has sounded good." – Thomas Sowell

"How many intentions have we seen realized, which have been pronounced impossible?" – Etienne-Jules Marey

"In theory, there is no difference in practice and theory. In practice there is." – Yogi Berra

"Courage is being scared to death, but saddling up anyway." – John Wayne

"Adversity doesn't build character, it reveals it." - James Lane Allen

"The impact of a life is more important than its length." – Dr. Logan Cummings

"Experience is the best teacher." – Adage in various forms dating back to Julius Caesar

Appendix B

Battle's Bullets for a Bountiful Life

- Common sense is critical at any time, but more so in chaotic times.

- What you do in the present will create a past that will greatly influence your opportunities and dreams in the future.

- Institutions come and go. The only thing that lasts are the relationships you make and what you learn from the experience.

- Treat other people's money (your prospects, customers and company) as you would your own.

- There is no such thing as a dumb question, just dumb answers.

- The only dog that can't learn a new trick is a dead dog.

- I will, is no substitute for I DID.

- If you don't manage your time, your time will manage you.

- Forward, always move forward.

- Life is not fair. It doesn't matter which party is running the government. Get over it!

- Everything you do today impacts your future.

  » If you want something tomorrow, invest today to earn it.
  » If you wanted something today, you should have invested efforts yesterday to earn it.

- If Hindsight is 20/20 and experience is the best teacher, why are young people who have neither always so quick to ignore the experience that is available from those who have both?

- It's bad luck to be superstitious.

- **Aim High!**
  Work Hard!
  NEVER Quit!

INDEX

Dallas Mavericks basketball team – 22-23

Dallas Morning News – 13

David, King of Israel – 32

Davis, Jim – 91

Dayton, Ohio – 21

Dell Computer – 5

Dell, Michael – 5-6

DeLorean - 67

Denver, Colorado – 202

Depression – 1930's – v,72,108,132,186

DeRossi, Joe – 146

Detroit Tigers – 174

Deuteronomy – 120

Disney, Walt – 20,82,222

Disneyland – 20

Disney World – 20

Disraeli, Benjamin – 34,222

Doolittle Raiders – 72

Doss, Desmond – 148,224

Dot.com bust – 115,144

Durant, William C. – 227

Eastwood, Clint – 116

Ecclesiastes – 46

Edison, Thomas – 82

Einstein, Albert – 6, 20,82,221,227

Emerson, Ralph Waldo – 83,223,225

Endurance – 72,222

England – 27,52,95

Egypt – 31, 135

Epictetus - 227

Estes, Billie Sol - 65

Eve – 45,64

Everything is Possible – 88

Fielder, Cecil – 175

Florida – 175

Formula One – 32

ABOUT THE AUTHOR
RICHARD V. BATTLE

MULTI AWARD-WINNING AUTHOR, SPEAKER AND ADVISOR

Richard has previously authored, *Conquering Life's Course – Common Sense in Chaotic Times, Unwelcome Opportunity: Overcoming Life's Greatest Challenges, The Master's Sales Secrets, The Four-Letter Word that Builds Character, Surviving Grief by God's Grace,* and *The Volunteer Handbook: How to Organize and Manage a Successful Organization.*

He has been a public speaker and trainer for over 30 years on topics including, leadership, motivation, faith, sales, and volunteerism.

Richard was an executive with **KeyTrak** (a Reynolds and Reynolds company), and has more than 40 years of experience in sales, executive management and leadership in various business entities.

He was **appointed by Texas Governor Rick Perry** to **The Texas Judicial Council** and **The Texas Emerging Technology Fund**.

As president of the **Austin Junior Chamber of Commerce** (1983-1984), the U.S. Junior Chamber of Commerce recognized the chapter as the Most Outstanding chapter in the United States, and the **Junior Chamber of Commerce International recognized Richard as the Outstanding Chapter President in the world**.

He served on the board of directors of **Alpha Kappa Psi**, international professional business fraternity, and was a past chairman.

He has served on the board of many organizations including **The John Ben Shepperd Public Leadership Foundation, Boy Scouts of America, Muscular Dystrophy Association** and **Keep Austin Beautiful**.

Richard lives in Lakeway, Texas. His mission is to communicate timeless messages of proven principles to help people win every day.

Richard V. Battle Resources

Conquering Life's Course
Common Sense in Chaotic Times

Do you wonder if Common Sense is vanishing?

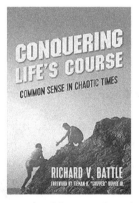

It will entertain and inspire the reader to think, laugh and undertake actions to realize a more fulfilling life.

If you or a loved one have given up on understanding the world of today, Conquering Life's Course is a must read. It offers reassurance to the reader that age-old traditions and wisdom still rule over unproven theory.

It is concise, easy-to-read and offers invaluable insights that can be shared with the whole family.

Reader Views – 1st Place – Self Help – 2019

CIPA EVVY Awards – 3rd Place – Self Help – 2020

Readers' Favorite – Finalist – Motivation/Inspiration - 2020

Available in paperback, Kindle, and audio editions.

Unwelcome Opportunity –
Overcoming Life's Greatest Challenges

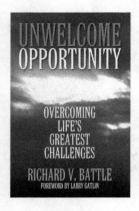

What do you do when you experience divorce, two heart procedures and a cancer diagnosis within ten months? It is the story of an ordinary man facing multiple life challenges in a ten-month period.

In it you will see an example of God's presence and provision that helped Richard Battle traverse this turbulent period of his life.

Readers Favorite – Gold Medal – Christian Devotion/Study - 2019

Reader Views – 2nd Place – Religion – 2019

Illumination Book Awards – Bronze Medal – Christian Living – 2020

Available in paperback, Kindle, Nook and audio editions.

Surviving Grief by God's Grace

There is no greater loss in this world than the loss of one's child. This book is the first-person account of the author's loss of his first and then only child. It is a story of the grief, spiritual quest and grace that helped Richard and his family survive, and to live with hope for the future.

Writer's Digest – Honorable Mention -Inspiration - 2003

Available in paperback and Kindle editions.

The Four-Letter Word That Builds Character

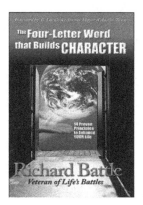

Why are so many young people having a problem adapting to society today? Where have we gone wrong? Is it the parents or society in general? The Four Letter Word That Builds Character can make a difference in this scattered and cluttered world. Based on the lessons learned from the author's first job and parental teaching of traditional values that have proven to be the foundation for lifelong success, this volume teaches 14 proven principles of a good work ethic and character.

USA Today's Best Books – Finalist – Business Motivation - 2006

Available in paperback Kindle and audio editions.

The Volunteer Handbook
How to Organize and Manage a Successful Organization

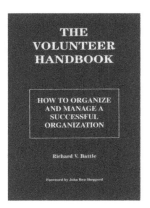

More than 75 topics that provide specific ideas that will help volunteer leaders maximize their efforts. Topics include: Long range, annual and event planning. Training board and prospective board members. How to recruit new members, 10 steps to activate or reactivate a member, 6 steps to building a successful team. How to motivate your membership. Effective Delegation. Managing non-performers.

Available in paperback

The Master's Sales Secrets
44 Strategies for Sensational Sales Success

Richard V. Battle offers business leaders a graduate-level class in what he's learned in over forty plus years in sales and sales management. Practical, sharp, and clearly communicated, The Master's Sales Secrets can be read cover to cover or referenced strategy by strategy.

Available in paperback and Kindle editions.

www.richardbattle.com

CPSIA information can be obtained
at www.ICGtesting.com
Printed in the USA
LVHW091844011220
673140LV00038B/260